Being Human In A World of Illusion

Karen & Charles
Thank you for all
your love + support
+ for being such
extraordinary people
and parents and for
giving your gifts so
freely + generously

love to all of you
Ruth

Being Human In A World of Illusion

Donald Theiss

ISBN: 1511489332
ISBN 13: 9781511489331

Table of Contents

CHAPTER 1

You are Perfect

———— ∞ ————

YOU ARE PERFECT, EXACTLY THE way you are, a perfect manifestation of the Universe happening, in the form of a human being.

We are all perfect, just as we are. Every aspect of our being is a perfect part of the Universe manifesting in human form, energetically and physically. Our eyes, ears, nose, brain, vagina, clitoris, penis, anus, breasts, nipples, liver, heart, glands, bones, nerves, feelings and sensations, are all perfect parts of the way we are designed to be by the energy of the Universe. We are all perfect manifestations of the Universe in the form of a human being and when we accept ourselves, exactly the way we are, we realize we are perfect exactly the way we are.

We are human beings living in a society that lives in and according to, socially fabricated beliefs about reality that reject how we really are and trains us to hide, suppress and reject how we really are and to pretend to be some way we are not, in order to fit into this socially fabricated conceptual illusion about how we should be. We are taught to suppress, hide and deny how we really are and to think and live according to these fabricated social beliefs about how we should be.

Our beliefs about how we should be play like a movie in our mind, distorting our perception of how we really are and causing us to suppress, reject and deny how we really are. When we think and live in these socially fabricated conceptual ideas about how we should be, they interfere with our ability to be who and how we really are and interfere in our ability to tune into what is happening in us and interfere with our ability to function fully, as human beings.

Reality is simply how something really is. Reality is how we really are, how our body is, how all of our parts function, mentally, emotionally and physically including all of our feelings, sensations, and perceptions, as they really are.

Our socially fabricated beliefs about how we should be are conceptual ideas, mental pictures about how we "think we should be" but they are not the reality of how we really are. Our socially fabricated conceptual beliefs have become our focus of attention, our view of reality and they are interfering with the reality of how we really are. We are living in a socially fabricated movie in our mind, about how we should be and we are preventing ourselves from seeing, being and accepting how we really are and this is preventing us from functioning fully as human beings.

We learn our beliefs from our society and are trained to think these socially fabricated beliefs are real and in the process of growing up in these beliefs, we develop our own individual version of these beliefs that fits into the beliefs of the culture around us.

Although these beliefs are not real, they do create our perception of reality, stimulating our thoughts, ideas, reactions, actions and in turn, our interactions with one another.

We are living in a socially fabricated movie of how we think we should be and we are pretending to be how we are taught to think we should be according to these socially fabricated beliefs. We play our part in the socially created movie, in order to fit into our society and these socially driven illusions that are distorting our awareness, our perceptions, our patterns of thought, our emotional reactions, our physiological responses and our behaviors and interactions with one another.

We have become actors in this socially fabricated movie, playing roles with one another rather than being real, rather than being who and how we really are, and this is preventing us from expressing who and how we really are, openly, honestly and authentically and this inability to be real is stimulating our distorted interactions with one another.

If we were capable of being real, of expressing ourselves openly and honestly, we could be having open, honest, authentic and truly connected experiences with one another. We have gotten so lost in the socially fabricated illusions, we have lost touch with our actual responses, with who we really are, with our self as we really are.

We are taught the ways and beliefs of our society and we learn to play our role in this socially fabricated movie and we become part of this way of seeing, being and relating.

Our learned socially fabricated beliefs, determine our perception of reality, how we see life, how we see our self, how we see others, what we accept, what we reject, and what we allow ourselves to feel, think and express to one another. We live in this socially fabricated illusion of how we should be and limit what we accept or allow ourselves to experience, show or express. We deny the truth of how we really are and follow these socially fabricated beliefs as if they are real and our real responses are not.

Our neurobiological system is designed perfectly to be exactly to function exactly the way it functions, by the design of the energy of the Universe. Our body, our feelings, our sensations and our perception are all aspects of the design of the Universe, in human form. Our neurobiological system is designed to be exactly the way it is and to function perfectly, physically, mentally, sensorily and emotionally.

We are only one form of organic life happening and we are perfect in every way, the way the energy of the Universe designed us to be. We are only one of an infinite variations of the Universe manifesting in physical form. We are physical, sensorial, emotional and mental beings and we do not fit into any socially fabricated belief about how we should be.

Beliefs are not real, they are only conceptual ideas, pictures in our mind about reality but they are not the reality of how we really are. Our beliefs are simply a description, a made up mental picture, an explanation about us and not the experience that we are actually having. We are the reality as we are and not these socially fabricated beliefs about us. Our beliefs about how we should be are simply ideas that we have been taught to believe.

We are trained to think there is something wrong with us, something wrong with our emotions, something wrong with our bodies, especially our sexual parts, our vagina, our penis, our breasts, our nipples and our anus. We are taught to hide our bodies, suppress our feelings and our sensations of pain and pleasure. We are taught to hide our vagina, penis, breasts, nipples and anus in the belief that these parts of us are bad, wrong or sinful. We are trained to hide and suppress our feelings, sensations, thoughts and our sexual responses and to fit ourselves into the socially fabricated beliefs of our society that these parts of us are bad.

We are born into this socially fabricated movie and we develop our own role in this social movie, hiding and suppressing our real self, hiding our body and suppressing our feelings and sensations and our own individual perceptions, our own individual experience and connection with reality. By living in and according to this socially fabricated belief about reality, we are cutting ourselves off from our own individual experience of reality and thus from being able to tune into the guidance that it is giving us and thus to function fully, as we are designed to function.

We can't really fit ourselves into these socially fabricated beliefs because they aren't real. They are only pictures in our mind, stories we were taught to tell ourselves that aren't the reality of our actual experience.

Reality is simply the way we really are. We have bodies with penises, vaginas, breasts and anuses, with sensations of pleasure and pain and emotions that react to what is happening in our environment that are guiding us in moving toward or away from something. We are the way we are designed to be by the energy of the Universe, with bodies, minds, sensations and feelings that are always moving in us and guiding us through life. We are the way we were created to be by the energy of the Universe, with bodies, feelings, sensations and perceptions that are always responding and guiding us through life if we pay attention to them and follow them.

We are designed to be how we are and we can't change how we are but we have been taught to deny, hide and suppress how we really are and this is distorting our perception, our reactions, our behaviors and our interactions with one another. We are human beings, living in a world of illusion and we are real but our socially fabricated beliefs about how we should be are not. We are human beings, living in a world of illusion.

CHAPTER 2

Beliefs

——⚬⚬⚬——

BELIEFS ARE SIMPLY IDEAS THAT we think over and over. Beliefs are conceptual notions about reality, conceptual ideas about reality, mental descriptions about reality, that are not the reality they describe. Like a picture of a bird on a chalk board, they are not real and they don't sing or fly and are just a picture of some part of reality but not reality, as it is.

Don Juan Matus said we are perceivers more that we are do-ers and how we perceive determines what we see and forms our view of reality. We have the ability to perceive with our whole being so that we can assess what is happening in us and around us and act in accordance with what we are perceiving so we can perceive what is happening in us and around us in order to deal with existence as effectively as we can.

The problem we are having is that we have been taught to perceive reality through these socially fabricated concepts about it, rather than perceiving reality directly with our own neuro-biological system and tuning into our own direct experience of reality as it is happening in us and around us.

We are taught to perceive reality through these socially fabri-cated pictures in our mind rather than through our own direct perception of what is actually happening. We are taught to perceive through these socially constructed pictures of reality, as if they are real and we are taught to ignore our own individual responses, as if they are not real.

We are taught to deny our own responses and follow these socially fabricated rituals of thought and behavior and to play a role within these socially fabricated belief structures, which sees us as flawed, physically, emotionally, mentally and sexually.

We live in a socially fabricated system of beliefs that teaches us to believe that our body is sinful and to think our emotions, our sensations and our biological functions, like orgasm, peeing and pooping are shameful and must be hidden and suppressed. We are taught to hide our body, especially our sexual parts and to suppress our feelings and sensations, in obedience to these false socially fabricated beliefs.

Most of us live according to these socially fabricated beliefs, as if they are real and as if there is something wrong with us, especially our sexuality, our emotions and any thing that makes us unique or different. We are real human beings but we are living in this world of illusion.

CHAPTER 3

The Belief That There is
Something Wrong With Us

———— ∞ ————

THE PRIMARY BELIEF ON OUR planet is that there is something wrong with us that we must suppress, hide and reject our self, in order to be good and acceptable. We are taught to hide our body, especially our sexual parts and to suppress our feelings and sensationsd in order to be acceptable to our societies fabricated beliefs. We have been taught to feel ashamed of our body, our feelings and especially our sexuality and this has created conflict in us between how we really are and how we are pretending to be to fit into these socially fabricated illusions.

These socially fabricated beliefs are perpetuated by everyone through indoctrination, conditioning and modeling. We grow up in this society observing people hiding their bodies and suppressing their feelings, thoughts, sensations and sexuality and we learn from watching them to hide our body and suppress our responses to fit into the society.

We try to follow these socially fabricated beliefs about how we should be because we want to fit in and be accepted but we can't because these beliefs are not real and we feel the conflict between these beliefs and how we really are. Our body, our emotions, our sensations and everything else about us is exactly the way it is designed to be by the Universe. We have a body with sensations, feelings and sexual parts and all of these parts and responses are flowing in us and through us continuously, regardless of these socially fabricated beliefs.

We are trained to hide, suppress and reject ourselves and thus be at odds with ourselves, with how we really are, with our actual way of being, with our real self, with our real feelings, thoughts, and sensations that are moving through our physical body.

In spite of all the socially fabricated beliefs about how we should be, we are the way we are, the way we are designed to be by the energy of the universe and that can't change because our socially fabricated beliefs say we should. We are not designed to be the way these socially fabricated beliefs say we should because these beliefs are not real; they are only ideas that some human being made up and taught the rest of us to believe.

In homage to these socially fabricated beliefs, we suppress and hide our feelings, sensations and our bodies and pretend to be the way these socially fabricated beliefs say we should be. We try to fit ourselves into these beliefs but we can't because they aren't real. We are real human beings, living in a world of illusion. We try to live according to these beliefs so we can fit in and get accepted but we are in conflict with how we really are and consequently we are in conflict with one another.

We get use to hiding, suppressing and denying how we really are and we lose our ability tune into our actual responses, to feel what we are really feeling or be aware of our own sensations and thoughts. We hide, suppress and inhibit our own responses and lose our ability to express what we are really experiencing, openly or honestly. We get so use to hiding and suppressing our real responses, we lose touch with our own feelings and sensations and this interferes with the functioning of our own neurobiological system.

When we suppress our feelings, sensations and thoughts, we are suppressing our own neurobiological system and preventing it from functioning. In the process we create conflict in our self which leads to tension, stress, dysfunction and breakdown in our own neurobiological system, at all levels of our being; mentally, emotionally and physically.

These socially fabricated beliefs are interfering with our ability to function mentally, emotionally and physically and our patterns of suppressing and hiding ourselves is interfering with our ability to express ourselves openly, honestly and authentically and thus preventing us from being able to connect with one another and create intimacy in our relationships.

Our patterns of suppressing, hiding and pretending are causing conflict in us and creating conflict in our relationships with one another. We create conflict within ourselves because we are suppressing ourselves and not accepting how we really are; our body, our feelings, our sensations, our thoughts, our sexuality, our individual fantasies, visions and our actual way of being.

This book is an attempt to help us see the truth of how we really are, as human beings and distinguish between how we really are and the socially fabricated ideas about how we should be.

My intention in writing this book is to make us aware of these socially fabricated beliefs and to support each of us in accepting ourselves as we really are and realizing that we are perfect the way we are and regaining our ability to be real and to express ourselves openly, honestly, fully and freely so that we can free ourselves to be how we really are with our self and with one another.

Werner Erhard once said, "a transformed person is a person who can tell the truth and a transformed society is one in which the truth can be told". I want all of us to learn to be real and to tell the truth of our own experience and I want us to create a society in which the truth can be told. When we accept our self as we really are, we can allow ourselves to feel our actual feelings and sensations and we can express ourselves fully and freely and create a society in which we can be real and express our truth openly and honestly.

Accepting our self, as we really are is the only way out of the fabricated illusions of our society and the only way out of the conflict we feel in our self and with one another. When we accept our self as we really are we are accepting the Universe the way it really is, in the form of a human being. When we accept our self, as we really are, we give our self permission to be how we really are, with all of our feelings, sensations, thoughts, images, fantasies, visions, including our physical body and it's sexual parts and sensations and in the process we accept and allow everyone else to do the same.

CHAPTER 4

Our Conditioned View of Reality

———— ∞∞∞ ————

WE ARE ALL CONDITIONED INTO a view of reality according to the prevailing beliefs of our society. We are indoctrinated into these socially fabricated beliefs by everyone because everyone in our society is indoctrinated into these same beliefs. We are all indoctrinated into these beliefs and we each develop our own individual interpretation of these beliefs and develop our role within this socially fabricated belief system. The beliefs into which we are born create our perceptions of reality, our reactions to reality and how we fit ourselves into the social world in which we live.

We are all indoctrinated into these beliefs, so we tend to see reality in a similar way and agree, to some extent, on our view of reality. Our socially learned beliefs create a picture in our mind of how we are supposed to be and these ideas determine our perceptions of reality, what we see, how we see, how we describe and interpret what we see and how we relate to our self and to one another.

We tend to see things in a similar way so how we see our self and others is similar. For instance, we are all trained to believe that there is something wrong with us or with certain aspects of us, especially our emotions and our sexuality, our penis, vagina, breasts, nipples, anus, so most of us feel uncomfortable with these parts of us. We are taught to hide and suppress our feelings and our sexuality so we feel uncomfortable with our feelings and our sexuality.

We are trained to believe there is something wrong with us and that there is a "right way" to be and a " wrong" way to be, so we argue over who is right and who is wrong. Consequently, we judge, criticize and reject our self and one another and blame our self and one another for being the way we are. We argue over who is right and who is wrong because we were trained to believe parts of us are wrong and therefor unacceptable so we argue over what we think is wrong with us or someone else.

We are trained to believe that sex is wrong, so we suppress our sexual responses and hide our sexual parts. When we feel sexual we also feel shame because we have been taught to think sex is wrong and that we are bad for being sexual. We are taught to believe sex is wrong so we try to hide and suppress our sexual energy in order to maintain an image of being good. We try to suppress our natural sexual energy so we are in conflict with ourselves when we feel a sexual response. When we respond sexually to one another we are afraid to be fully open, honest or expressive of our responses because we are trained to think sex is wrong and to be ashamed of our sexuality. When we do have a sexual response we hide it, suppress it and pretend something else is happening, talk about something else, how nice we look or what we think about current issues rather than expressing our real responses to one another. We are not allowed by prevailing social beliefs to express our sexuality openly, honestly or freely, so we hide and suppress our sexual responses and in the process we disconnect from our real responses, from our self and from one another.

CHAPTER 5

Imposition of Beliefs

———— ⌘ ————

THE GREAT TYRANNY OF HUMAN kind is the imposition of these socially fabricated beliefs. We impose socially fabricated beliefs on one another, as we hide and suppress our own responses and stifle ourselves by restricting what we allow ourselves to feel and express. This is devastating to us individually and to our relationships with one another.

The socially fabricated beliefs into which we have been indoctrinated teach us that we are wrong for being the way we are. The imposition of these socially fabricated beliefs is justified by claiming these beliefs come from God, even though when we really look at this we can see that all beliefs are made up by human beings and not by God.

We are trained to think these beliefs are good and we are taught to impose them on one another as part of the belief that they are good and the right way to be according to these beliefs.

These socially fabricated beliefs in right and wrong are used as the basis for all imposition of beliefs on one another. When we impose our beliefs on one another, we are acting out of the belief that our beliefs are right and that we have a right to force these beliefs on everyone. We do this in our most intimate relationships, with our children, our wives, our husbands, our friends and families and wonder why we are in such conflict in our self and with one another and why we can't seem to get our relationships to work or develop into truly intimate relationships.

We reinforce these socially fabricated beliefs and patterns of thought and behavior because we are all indoctrinated into these beliefs and although they are similar, we each develop our own individual version of the prevailing social beliefs and try to get one another to agree with our particular view, which creates all the conflicts we experience in our relationships.

We learn to play a role in the socially fabricated belief system rather than learning to be how we really are and simply express our own individual experience.

We aren't usually aware that we are playing a role or presenting a social image over top of our real responses because we are so use to doing it. We can see when others are playing a role and we think to ourselves, "She is so fake, he is such a game player" but we don't see that we are doing the same thing and not being real when we are showing or expressing something other than what we are actually feeling or thinking. We see the pretensions of others but not our own because our patterns of thought and behavior have become unconscious and invisible to us.

We argue over our particular versions of the socially fabricated beliefs, thinking our beliefs are right and other peoples beliefs are wrong. We don't usually see that beliefs are just conceptual ideas borrowed from our society and not the reality of how we really are. We argue over who's version of the socially fabricated illusion is right but we are arguing over fabricated concepts about reality, while we are not even in touch with our own experience of reality.

All of our arguments are about our different views of the socially fabricated beliefs about reality and none of it is reality. Our beliefs are nothing more than conceptual ideas about reality that we have come to believe are real.

We live in our own socially fabricated movie about reality, about how we should be, about how others should be, about how life should be, while we hide and suppress the actual experiences we are having. We live inside our own mental version of our socially learned beliefs and the social movie in which we are participating.

Our own personal illusion is our version of the social illusion, the movie that we collectively create and perpetuate through our own participation in it. We relate to one another according to our learned beliefs and patterns of thought and behavior, the rules of behavior they dictate and the role we have develop in this social movie. We live our lives as if our beliefs are real and as if we are being real, while we play a role in the social movie and deny how we really are.

The problem we are having as individuals, as well as a society, is that our beliefs are not real and do not represent how we really are and they are interfering with us being who we really are and this is preventing us from being fully functional and this is causing conflict in our self and in our relationships with one another.

Our beliefs are preventing us from being how we really are, from being real with one another and this interferes with our ability to connect with our self or one another. We hunger for real connection while we suppress and hide ourselves and prevent ourselves from seeing or being seen and having the intimacy we desire. Our beliefs are in the way of us being who we really are or accepting ourselves as we really are and from being able to express ourselves openly, honestly or authentically.

Our socially fabricated beliefs are concepts about reality, our pictures, our ideas, the movie in our mind about reality and we are all trying to fit ourselves into to these illusions. Our beliefs are perceptual illusions into which we have become mesmerized and they are causing us to separate from our actual experience and preventing us from connecting with our real self and with one another.

CHAPTER 6

Patterns of Thought and Behavior

———— ✺ ————

PATTERNS OF THOUGHT AND BEHAVIOR develop in our mind, our emotions and our body and become unconscious and invisible to us
over time. We create a picture in our mind of who we are supposed to be according to these socially fabricated beliefs and act
out this picture in our lives, pretending to be the way we think
we should be, in order to fit into our society. In the process, we
lose conscious awareness of our real self, our real responses as
they are happening in us, below the surface of our awareness.

In living in a picture of how we think we should be and pretending responses that are different than the ones we are actually having, we develop patterns of hiding and suppressing our
real responses and lose our ability to connect with what we are
really sensing, feeling and thinking and our ability to express
ourselves openly, honestly and authentically. We lose our conscious awareness of our own sensations, feelings, thoughts and
images that are always happening within us, that are trying to
guide us in choosing what is in harmony with who we really are.

Our neurobiological systems are designed to respond to everything that is happening in us and around us, giving us signals in the form of feelings, sensations, thoughts and images

to guide us in making choices that are in alignment with us, in each and every situation in our life but when we hide and suppress them we are out of touch with our own responses, and disconnected from the neurobiological system that is guiding us.

We have gotten lost in our socially fabricated beliefs and our learned patterns of thought, reaction and behavior that are generated by our learned conceptual ideas about who we think we should be and have lost touch with our real responses. We are stuck in a socially fabricated belief system that has taught us to deny our real self, in favor of these socially fabricated ideas. We have been taught to hide, suppress and deny our own responses and are therefor in conflict with our actual responses and therefor our own inner guidance system and this is causing our mental, emotional, physical and relational disfunction.

CHAPTER 7

The Oppression of Beliefs

———— ❦ ————

We are all oppressed by these socially fabricated beliefs that deny how we really are, and are imposing these limiting beliefs on all of us through indoctrination and conditioning that teach us to hide and suppress our real responses.

From the time we are born we are taught to hide our bodies and suppress our responses and to pretend socially acceptable responses, according to the socially fabricated beliefs about how we are taught to believe we should be and how we should feel, think and act. We are pressured with reward and punishment into suppressing our real responses and pretending to be the way we are told we should be. We are taught to hide our bodies and to suppress our sensations and emotions that are our neurobiological system giving us messages and trying to guide us in making choices that are in harmony with what is most beneficial to who we are.

We are all indoctrinated into these socially fabricated beliefs, so we all think, react and behave according to them, participate in them and follow them in our relating with one another. We all operate according to these beliefs and model these beliefs in our attitudes, our perceptions, the way we speak, what we express and don't express, and what we show to one another.

We each learn to play our part in the socially fabricated illusions and integrate ourselves into these socially fabricated beliefs and play a role in the social movie that is created by these beliefs. We believe these beliefs are good so we play our role in the social movie and model these beliefs through our actions for our children and one another.

Our relationships are based on our beliefs and the role we have learned to play in the social movie and our thinking and behaviors are creating the way we relate to one another. We play socially fabricated games with one another that are based on our learned beliefs and our patterns of hiding, suppressing and pretending over top of what we are really sensing, feeling and thinking. This causes us to be disconnected from our actual responses and lose awareness of what we are really feeling, sensing and seeing and consequently, we lose our ability to show and express what we are really feeling and sensing and this prevents us from relating with one another openly, honestly or authentically and this prevents us from creating any real connection, any real intimacy, with one another.

We have become lost in the socially fabricated movie in our mind and the role we are playing in this socially created movie and have lost connection to our real self. When we play a role, rather than being real, we lose touch with our real responses and come to believe the role we are playing is who we really are. Like an actor in a movie, we act out our role in the socially fabricated movie and come to believe our role is who we really are.

We become mesmerized by our own mind movie and our own patterns of thought, reaction and behavior, while suppressing and hiding our real responses and pretending responses that fit into the social movie.

We have been taught to believe that there is something wrong with our bodies, our emotions and our sexuality and that we are wrong for having these parts of us. We have been taught to think we are wrong for being emotional or sexual so we hide and suppress and feel ashamed of being emotional or sexual.

We are taught to be afraid of our real responses, so we hide, suppress and pretend and cling to these socially fabricated beliefs and behaviors because they secure our place in the social group. We live in a continuous process of hiding, suppressing, pretending and denying who and how we really are in order to get the acceptance of others.

We try to fit ourselves into these beliefs about how we should be" and lose our ability to center in our own experience, accept our own experience and allow our own experience to guide us in our choices and actions in our own life.

We are human beings, living in a world of socially fabricated illusions, a social movie about how we should be, that isn't real and teaches us to deny our real self. Our indoctrination into hiding, suppressing and denying our real responses and pretending something else is causing us to dissociate from who we really are and these conceptual beliefs are in the way of us accepting how we really are and from living our lives fully, freely and functionally.

CHAPTER 8

The Social Illusion

———— ✺ ————

WE ALL GROW UP IN the socially fabricated illusions of our society. Socially established beliefs dominate our thinking, our emotional reactions, our behavior and our way of interacting with one another. We grow up in the social movie not realizing that we are in a movie that is invisible to us and we have gotten so use to playing our role in this social movie, we actually think the movie is real and that we are being real.

We play our role unconsciously and automatically, without awareness of what we are doing and because we are so used to playing our role, we think we are being real. This is what we were trained to do, what we learned to do and it is what we have been doing throughout our lives and it is what we are all doing right now, in this moment, in this situation, with everyone in our lives.

We are all taught to believe there is something wrong with us, so we hide, suppress and inhibit what we are really experiencing to fit into this socially programmed way of being. We pretend to be something we are not and spend much of our time and energy trying to figure out what's wrong with us, so we can fix our self, change our self and improve our self, so that we can finally be okay and fit into the socially fabricated movie.

We work on our self constantly, trying to be okay, trying to be better, trying to get better, trying to be good, trying to change our self, so we can fit in and get the acceptance and approval of the people around us, who share these same false ideas about reality. We try to change our self but nothing works because there is nothing wrong with us in the first place so we get lost in the socially fabricated belief that there is something wrong with us and continue to play our social games.

We are the way we are by the design of the Universe and we are perfect in every way, exactly the way we are. There is nothing wrong with us, there never was and there never will be. We are perfect the way we are, the way we were designed to be, sexually, emotionally, mentally, and physically

We were taught to believe there is something wrong with us, so we feel uncomfortable with ourselves; with our bodies, our minds, our sexuality and our feelings, when they don't fit into these socially fabricated illusions of how we should be. We feel bad about ourselves because we were taught to feel bad about ourselves, especially our emotions and our sexuality, these parts of us that are so natural and so fundamental to being a human being, these parts of us that brings us so much pleasure and profound connection with one another.

We are taught to judge, criticize, ridicule, threaten, intimidate, abuse and reject our self and others for being the way we really are and to judge our self and reject parts of ourselves, especially our sexuality and act out these same beliefs and attitudes toward our self and others. We learn these patterns of thought and behavior and play them out in our relationships with one another.

We all want to be loved and accepted for who we really are and we also want to fit in so we hide and suppress our real responses and pretend to be the way we were taught to believe we should be, just to fit in. We hide our body, suppress our feelings and pretend to be the way we were taught we should be and feel bad about who and how we really are.

We are controlled by these socially fabricated teachings that have taught us to control ourselves through suppressing, hiding and inhibiting our own natural neurobiological responses; our feelings, sensations, images, thoughts and visions.

Social indoctrination begins at birth and continues throughout our lives. Our parents are our first role models just as their parents were their first role models. We are conditioned and indoctrinated into the prevailing socially fabricated beliefs and we pass them on to each new baby born.

We learn these beliefs and integrate them into our own thinking, reacting, behaving and relating to one another. We imitate our parents as they did theirs, following the beliefs, attitudes, energy, facial expressions, emotions and every word they say and how they say it. We imitate their patterns of hiding and suppressing their feelings, sensations and thoughts and the way they express their own responses. We imitate their beliefs, their patterns of hiding, their patterns of suppressing, their shame, their guilt, their patterns of embarrassment, their inhibition and their socially learned ways of expressing themselves. This is the way socially fabricated beliefs are passed on from generation to generation, each generation indoctrinating the next into these socially fabricated beliefs and patterns of thought and behavior.

The problem we are having is that these socially fabricated beliefs are not real and are interfering with our natural way of being and are preventing us from allowing our own neurobiological system from functioning fully and freely. We are causing our own conflict and our own problems by suppressing our own neurobiological system from functioning the way it was designed to function.

Socially fabricated beliefs about what is good and bad are taught to us so we will control ourselves by suppressing our natural responses and fitting ourselves into the socially fabricated view of reality. We are taught to hide and suppress our self and to believe that suppressing and hiding is good and that we are being good when we hide and suppress our own natural way of being and our natural responses, especially our sexuality and our emotions.

One of my earliest memories of my own indoctrination into the social beliefs came in the form of my father's angry reaction to me hanging on my mother's leg, wanting her to nurse me when I was about two. She was nursing my sister and I wanted some too. He yelled at me from across the room, in an angry and threatening way "stop bothering your mother, leave her alone" I felt fear, anger and threatened, silenced my self and clung to my mother.

My father used anger to threaten us and teach us to control ourselves. If he didn't like something we were doing whether we were making noise, singing, jumping around, being silly, crying, laughing, expression feelings, he yelled in a way that was threatening and intimidating to condition us into suppressing ourselves and behaving according to his demands.

I didn't know I was being trained to suppress my feelings, my needs, my wants and my own expression of those needs. He threatened me to teach me to suppress my own responses and to follow his commands. He had been taught this way by his father and was simply passing on what he had been taught. This is the way we are all taught to deny our real responses and to follow the demands and expectations of others.

My mother and father had learned to hide their bodies and suppress their feelings and sexual responses by their society and they trained us to do the same. They lived in a society that believed the body is sinful and must be hidden and that feelings and sexuality are sinful and must be suppressed, in order to be good. They kept their bodies hidden and suppressed their real responses, only expressing themselves in an inhibited way, a limited way that was allowed by the socially fabricated beliefs and rules of their society. They expressed only what was considered polite and acceptable in their society.

Socially fabricated beliefs are taught and modeled by everyone in our society, including our brothers, sisters, aunts, uncles and everyone else in the community because we are all trained in the same beliefs. We all learn to hide our bodies and to suppress our sexuality, our feelings, our thoughts, our visions, our fantasies, our wants, our needs and our desires. We are all indoctrinated into the same beliefs, so we all develop similar patterns of thought, reaction and behavior, which is why we all think that hiding and suppressing is normal.

I had another experience when I was around five. My sister who was 4 and I were playing naked in the little cabin near our house. We were just playing and enjoying ourselves, when my older brother came in, saw we were naked and said, in a threatening way, "you better put some clothes on. I won't tell Mom and Dad this time". We had no idea we were doing anything "wrong" but we got the idea from my brother's attitude and energy. He was simply transferring the socially fabricated belief that being naked was bad and wrong onto us as it had been given to him. This was part of our conditioning and indoctrination into the beliefs of our society.

We were being trained to hide our bodies and to think there is something wrong with being naked and to feel fear and shame for being naked. My brother was just expressing what he had been taught about being naked. He was expressing the socially fabricated belief that being naked is bad, wrong and sinful and that we should hide our bodies from one another, to be good. He had learned this belief in the society around him and he was simply passing on what he had learned.

When I was seven I had another experience of indoctrination into this socially fabricated belief. A bunch of the kids from the neighborhood were playing strip poker and I lost all of my clothes first. I stood up, pulled down my underwear, opened my arms wide and proudly said, "see". The older kids, laughed and in unison, yelled "see", in a mocking tone. I felt ashamed and embarrassed, being ridicule for being naked again, indoctrinating me into the belief that there is something wrong with my naked body. The older kids were simply passing on the socially fabricated beliefs and attitudes they had learned from the world around them. Through ridicule they were passing on their learned sense of shame and embarrassment about their bodies. They had been taught these beliefs and had become part of the beliefs and part of the indoctrination into these beliefs. They showed their conditioned views, through ridicule of me for being naked. They were just doing what they had learned to do and were passing it on.

This kind of indoctrination continues throughout our lives, in many forms. In seventh grade I was suspended from school because I wore jeans in defiance of a school rule that jeans were not allowed. I argued that I had a right to wear jeans, as part of my right to life, liberty, and the pursuit of happiness and my inalienable right of free expression, granted by the U.S. Constitution.

I was expelled from school and ostracized by my peers who were afraid of being associated with me because I was bad for not obeying the rules. This was part of my indoctrination into the social system of control. We are told what to believe and do and we are attacked and rejected if we do not comply. I was scarred, intimidated and ashamed of being suspended, exiled, rejected and ostracized from school, from my peers and from my social world.

After a few weeks the principal came to my house and offered to buy dress pants if my parents would get me to wear them. My parents agreed and made a deal. I felt embarrassed and manipulated into doing what they wanted me to do, rather than what I felt was right for me and again I was being conditioned into the social rules by someone who had power to control through intimidation, threat and exclusion.

At 15, I was dragged down the school hallway by the assistant principal because I had the second button of my shirt open and my collar up. He considered this hoodlum dress and believed he was justified in attacking me because I did not fit into his idea about what was acceptable. He was bigger than me and used his size and strength to grab me and intimidate me into doing what he believed was right. I was being indoctrinated with abuse and intimidation into the social belief system and it's conceptual notions about what is right and what is wrong.

I experienced similar forms of indoctrination in the US Army when I was charged with conduct unbecoming, for drawing a picture of a naked woman. The post commander, a religious man, was offended and believed he was justified in punishing me for offending his belief. The beliefs of our society are imposed on us everyday by almost everyone in power, using intimidation and abuse to accomplish the goal of control.

Our social institutions, our schools, religions, governments, and other social institutions indoctrinate us into the prevailing beliefs of our society and we learn to fit ourselves into these beliefs, as best we can and when we don't adhere to the prevailing beliefs we are threatened, intimidated, abused, rejected and excluded.

Galileo was threatened with death by the leaders of the Catholic church when he expressed his observation that the earth revolves around the Sun and not the other way around. He was threatened with death and forced to publicly deny what he knew to be true, in order to keep from being murdered by the church.

We are all controlled in a similar manner by the institutions of our society with intimidation, threats and abuse into adhering to the prevailing beliefs of our society. Like Galileo, we deny our own experience, our own truth, what we know to be true, to protect our self from the abuse of others.

We are threatened into suppressing our real responses and we suppress ourselves to avoid the abuse and hostility we face if we don't. "I'll give you something to cry about". "Do what you are told". "Shut up and sit down" are common phrases used in my childhood to intimidate us into doing what we were told.

Our social institutions control us by teaching us to control ourselves through hiding, suppression and inhibition of our own responses. We live in a state of tension between the reality of our real responses and the social roles we are taught to play, to avoid abuse and rejection from the world around us. We want to be accepted and we are afraid of being rejected, so we hide and suppress our real responses and show only what is allowed, just like Galileo.

CHAPTER 9

Psychological and Physiological Effects of Suppressing Our Real Responses

———— ✦ ————

SUPPRESSION OF OUR NATURAL RESPONSES has a negative effect on our mind, emotions and body. When we suppress our responses we are stopping the energy that is moving through us in a contracted state, a state of tension. Suppressing our energy, amplifies what is being held back and builds in intensity in us, requiring more tension, mentally, emotionally and physically to hold it in. As tension builds in our system we create higher levels of stress in ourselves and this in turn causes us and our system to break down and dysfunction mentally, emotionally and physically.

Our feelings of love, fear, hurt, anger, sadness, and sexuality do not go away because we suppress them. Our mental, emotional and physical responses are all part of our neurobiological system, doing what it is designed to do, functioning the way it is designed to function and when we block it by suppressing our own responses, we interfere with our own neurobiological system in doing what it is designed to do. Our neurobiological system is designed to respond with feelings, sensations, images and thoughts as a way of signaling us and guiding us in our interactions with everyone and everything in our world.

The tension we create by suppressing our sensations, feelings and thoughts causes stress which creates inflammation, which leads to pain, suffering and dysfunction and disease in all it's many forms. When we suppress our own responses, we live in a mental, emotional, physical state of conflict with our self.

We are in a state of tension with our self and trying to figure out what is wrong with us and what we need to do to fix ourselves, not realizing that we are causing our own conflict because we are suppressing our own natural responses.

This is a circular process of thinking there is something wrong with us, suppressing our own responses that we think are what's wrong with us, stimulating tension and stress and then thinking this is proof that there is in fact, something wrong with us. We think there is something wrong with us and this dominates our thinking, reactions and behavior, creating tension and we lose touch with our own natural responses that are always happening below the surface. What is really happening in us is hidden and suppressed by these socially fabricated ideas that are creating our conflict.

Our constant state of suppression stimulates a constant state of disturbance in the form of conflict with our own natural responses. We create the conflict and bring that conflicted energy into all of our relationships. What we don't accept in our self, we don't accept in others either, so we are in a constant state of disturbance with our self and others.

We reject our own thoughts, feelings, sensations, desires, fantasies, dreams and visions because we don't accept them or allow ourselves to experience them, freely, without the conflict.

We don't accept our self the way we are, so we hide, suppress and reject ourselves, try to control and deny our feelings, thoughts and sensations and pretend over top of all of it as it is happening. Our natural responses build up in intensity and eventually we feel overwhelmed with them. We swing from suppression of our responses to intense emotional reactions that explode out of us like a storm or implode in us causing a breakdown in our relationships or in ourselves. We control our emotions until the tension builds up and we have an emotional explosion and release the energy into ourselves or onto one another.

When we live in a continual state of suppression and tension, over long periods of time we become scattered, unable to focus and we develop symptoms of disease, in the form of headaches, stomach aches, muscle aches, organ dysfunction, heart attacks, strokes, cancer and other maladies of mind and body.

Suppression of our responses creates tension, tension creates stress, stress creates inflammation and inflammation creates dysfunction and disease.

We suppress ourselves to avoid the confrontation we would face if we expressed ourselves openly and honestly out of fear of rejection and abuse which determines the degree to which we suppress or rebel. If we are afraid someone is going to abuse us, we do not feel free to be how we really are or to express our real feelings, thoughts or sensations openly, honestly or authentically so we develop patterns of behavior to hide and suppress our real responses.

Our parents were conditioned to hide and suppress them-selves, so they were simply passing on what they were trained to do. This is the real meaning of the 'sins of the father " teaching. We are trained to follow the conceptual beliefs of our society and to deny our own responses. We don't realize we are sup-pressing our self and we pass these behaviors on to our chil-dren, unconsciously.

We see young children suppressing their feelings by tensing and holding their breath and contracting against what is try-ing to come out of them in response to a parent telling them to, "stop that crying or I'll give you something to cry about" or some such threat.

The socially fabricated beliefs of our society are not real, healthy or good but they are our societies patterns of thought and behavior and we inherited them from our society.

The socially fabricated beliefs are false perceptions of reality appearing to be real, which is the true definition of an illusion. These socially fabricated beliefs have become our beliefs and they are in the way of us accepting ourselves the way we really are and this is causing us to hide ourselves, suppress ourselves and reject ourselves as we really are.

We suppress our own responses because we have been taught to believe they are bad and we are bad for having them. We live within these socially fabricated beliefs and like Galileo, conform to the beliefs of our society, in order to protect ourselves from abuse by almost everyone in our society.

We hide, suppress, inhibit, and pretend to be different than we are, we separate from our real self and consequently, from one another. We hide and suppress our real responses and play a role, to fit into the illusions of our society.

We develop our individual role in this social matrix and become a part of the illusions of our society. We suppress our real responses behind a screen of pretense and play our part in the social illusion into which we were born. We are real but the role we are playing is not. We are trained to believe, think and see only what we are told to see, think and believe and yet, we continue to be how we are, having our own individual experience. We are human beings, living in a world of illusion.

CHAPTER 10

Beliefs Are Concepts

———— ∞∞ ————

BELIEFS ARE CONCEPTS IN OUR mind, ideas we think are reality but they are mental constructs and not the actual reality of our own experience. Our beliefs are ideas about life and not life as it is. We may have a belief about how we should be but we can never be the way we think we should be because our beliefs are just thoughts and not the reality of our actual way of being and the responses we are actually having.

We are life happening in the form of a human being, pulsing, vibrating sensations and feelings, in response to life and we are each having our own experience of this thing we call life. We are organic beings, living in a physical body, a neurobiological system with senses, feelings, thoughts and images that are stimulated in us to guide us through life. We are each having our own responses that guide us and they don't fit into anyone's beliefs about how we are supposed to be.

Our beliefs are only pictures of life, like a chalk drawing of a bird on a chalk board, it is not a bird and our belief about how we should be is not the reality of how we really are.

We are one of the many and varied manifestations of the energy of the Universe, in human form and we are exactly the way we are designed to be by this energy. We do not fit into any belief about how we should be. Our physical bodies are designed to be exactly the way they are, with nipples, vaginas, penises and sexual energy, emotions and sensations.

We are real but our beliefs are not. They are just conceptual ideas that we learned from our society. We can't fit our self into our beliefs because they are mental concepts about life and not real life, as it is. Like a chalk drawing of a bird, our beliefs are only mental pictures on the chalk board of our mind, they don't fly, sing or breath with the energy of life.

We feel conflict because we are at odds with our real self because we learned to think we should be the way our fabricated social beliefs say we should be. We feel conflict and tension because we do not accept ourselves as we really are and we are trying to be some way we are not, while we suppress and hide how we really are. We are in conflict because we do not accept our self the way we really are and we are suppressing and hiding our real feelings, sensations and thoughts behind a wall of pretense.

We are a living, breathing, neurobiological system with feelings, thoughts and sensations and the energy moving through us is the reality of how we and our neurobiological system is responding to life.

CHAPTER 11

Oppression, Suppression, Repression, Depression

———— ∞∞∞ ————

OPPRESSION, SUPPRESSION, REPRESSION AND DEPRESSION follow from one to another and are all part of what we human beings are doing to ourselves because we follow these fabricated beliefs of our society.

We are oppressed by these socially fabricated beliefs that teach us to suppress ourselves in order to avoid abuse and suppression of our feelings and sensations eventually becomes automatic and we are then repressed and if we continue repressing ourselves over a long period of time we can become depressed.

Oppression is imposition, forcing something on another, suppression is holding something in, repression is an unconscious pattern of suppression and depression is a complete flatlining of our emotions.

When we are being oppressed we feel fear and contract because of the threat of being harmed in some way, so we hide and suppress ourselves to avoid harm and if we do this long enough we develop a pattern of suppressing that we call repression.

Our unconscious patterns of repressed thoughts, feelings and sensations causes our neurobiological system to automatically block what we are feeling and we lose touch with our own experience.

Every child born goes through indoctrination and conditioning into these socially fabricated beliefs, training us to hide and suppress through a process of reward and punishment, using threats, intimidation and abuse to train us into limiting our expression of anything that is unacceptable to the prevailing beliefs of our society.

We are oppressed with threats and abuse and we suppress to avoid abuse and rejection by parents, teachers, governments, police, religious leaders and almost everyone else in our society.

We develop patterns of repression and lose awareness of what we are actually feeling, sensing or thinking and when we no longer feel our feelings and sensations we are depressed and our neurobiological system has shut down and is no longer able to function. Depression is the flat lining of our sensory and emotional responses, the numbed state of our neurobiological system after years of suppressing our real responses. When we are depressed, we look emotionally dead, our face looks blank and we feel numb on the inside. This is not caused by a chemical imbalance but rather by the training we receive to suppress our own responses.

We are born a fully functioning neurobiological system with feelings, thoughts and sensations, designed to respond to our environment and guide us in fulfilling our wants, needs and desires in order to survive. We are driven by our sensations, feelings and mental images to act, move, touch, suck, coo and cry, in our interactions with everyone and everything in our environment in the process of getting our needs met. Our feelings, sensations, and mental activity are our neurobiological system responding and guiding us toward the fulfillment of our needs.

We were all created with sexual parts that are designed to feel pleasurable sensations in them, so that we will touch one another sexually and come together to enjoy the pleasures of sex and in the process create new life and all of this is designed by the energy of the Universe.

Our society trains us to suppress our neurobiological responses and to follow beliefs about what we should feel and think according to "the prevailing socially fabricated beliefs about what is good." We are trained to suppress our natural responses and to follow the rules of the prevailing social belief system in order to avoid negative reactions from others who have been trained in the same false beliefs. In the process, we internalize these socially fabricated beliefs and follow them in our thinking, acting and interacting with one another. The prevailing social beliefs are forced on us, through conditioning and indoctrination and we learn to suppress our real responses, to avoid abuse and rejection.

Most of us live in this pattern of unconscious repression, most of the time, unaware of what we are actually feeling as we learn to function in the world, while our real feelings, sensations and thoughts remain hidden beneath our learned social patterns of pretended behaviors.

If our patterns of repression become so complete and automatic that we are no longer able to feel our feelings and sensations, we are described as depressed. Depression is simply the 'flat lining" of our feelings and sensations so completely that we are numb and out of touch with the energy that is moving in us. Depression is the result of many years of oppression, suppression and repression. We do not become depressed because of some chemical imbalance. We become depressed because we have been trained to suppress our responses so completely that our neurobiological system simply shuts down. Chemical imbalances come from depression of our neurobiological system and not the other way around. This is like contracting a muscle until the muscle atrophies.

CHAPTER 12

Natural Design

———⟨⟨⟩⟩———

WE ARE ALL PART OF the design of the Universe. We are the energy of the Universe in human form just as our cells are a part of our body and are our body. We are cells in the Universe and at the same time, we are the Universe. We are not separate from the whole, we are the cells that make up the whole.

We argue over who's view of the Universe is right but our views are just views, ideas we make up to explain it to ourselves. Each of us is part of the Universe happening, in human form. We are life happening. We are existence happening. We are the Universe happening in physical form, with bodies, sensations, feelings and thoughts and we are designed to feel, sense, perceive and express, as part of the process of being alive in a physical body.

Our responses are our neurobiological system responding and giving us signals from our own body, guiding us toward what is beneficial for us and away from what is not. We are designed with bodies, sensations, feelings and thoughts to let us know what is happening and what action to take in response. This is our own personal neurobiological feedback system guiding us toward what is right for us in each situation.

Our thoughts, feelings and sensations are all part of our natural way of being. We are life happening and all of our responses are part of this experience that we are having. We are designed to have responses in the form of sensations, feelings and thoughts as part of how we function and when we allow our responses to move freely and allow ourselves to feel, follow and express all that is moving through us, we are being fully functional and alive.

We are not designed to suppress, hide or deny what we are feeling, thinking or sensing. Suppression is not natural. Suppression is a socially created behavior that we learn in order to avoid abuse and rejection by our society. Suppressing our energy is against who we really are, against our own energy, against our own self, against the way we really are, against life, against nature, against the Universe, against God and against our own neurobiological system, the way it is designed to be.

We are the way we are by the design of the Universe and we function the way we are designed to function but we have been trained by our society to deny our natural way of being and this training is interfering with our ability to be who we are and to function fully.

We are designed to feel, sense, think and respond to what is happening in us and around us, as a natural part of interacting with the world around us. Our whole physical body is designed to be the way it is and when we hide and suppress our responses, we stop our own neurobiological response mechanism from functioning fully.

Researchers at both Johns Hopkins and Brigham Young have concluded that when we develop a pattern of tension we create inflammation in our body which leads to dysfunction and the breakdown of the physical body, which we call disease. Researches have concluded that inflammation is caused by tension and is the fundamental cause of all disease and tension is the result of the conflict that we create when we suppress our own neurobiological system.

When we suppress ourselves, tension builds and we feel agitated and disturbed mentally, emotionally and physically. The disturbance we feel is our own neurobiological system giving us signals to make a change and if we don't make a change, the signal gets louder until we explode or implode and are forced to change. When we block our own responses, we block our own energy and we block our own internal feedback system and eventually we create a problem in our own system.

Our dysfunction shows up physically, mentally and emotionally. When we suppress our responses, we create conflict in our own system and we feel disturbed, anxious and tense. We may have difficulty thinking clearly, learning or retaining information. We may have trouble relating to the people around us because we are hiding and suppressing ourselves because we are afraid of being seen, abused and rejected. We may feel confused and unable to understand what is happening in us or around us, especially in our most intimate relationships.

When we suppress our real responses, we separate ourselves from our own responses and focus on the movie in our mind about how we should be. The movie in our mind is not real or connected with our real responses and is a disconnected version of our individual experience of reality. We are disconnected from our real responses and this is what creates the conflict and confusion in us and consequently in our relationships with one another.

We try to understand and define the dysfunctions we are experiencing in our mind and body in strictly physical terms, as if the breakdowns in our mind and body are being caused by some chemical imbalance. We define the breakdown in medical or psychological terms, like ADHD, bipolar, neurosis, psychosis, cancer, headaches, heart attacks, strokes, but the real source of these malfunctions of body and mind is the conflict we are creating in ourselves because we do not accept how we really are.

We have to understand the origins of our dysfunction in order to resolve the problem and become fully functional again and the real source of our conflicts is the suppression of our own neurobiological system.

We argue over the cause of our dysfunctional patterns, thinking they are caused by "chemical imbalances" or some physiological source but the real source is the suppression of our own energy, our own responses and the consequent interference with the functioning of our neurobiological system.

When we suppress our responses, we are blocking the flow of our own energy and this is creating a tug of war in us, between our actual responses and our socially learned pretended responses.

We are trained to think that there is something wrong with us, so we hide and suppress ourselves and try to figure out what is wrong with us, so we can fix it, correct it, hide it and find some way to feel okay with our self. There is nothing wrong with us in the first place, so there is nothing to correct or fix but because we believe there is, we live in constant conflict with our self and consequently, with one another.

We are trying to fit ourselves into a socially fabricated illusion and trying to be the way we were trained to think we "should be," while we are hiding and suppressing ourselves and not accepting ourselves or allowing ourselves to be how we really are. We pretend to feel good, to feel okay, over top of our thoughts that we are not okay because we aren't the way we are trained to believe we should be and we can't because we can't fit our real self into these socially fabricated illusions.

CHAPTER 13

Fear of Our Responses

———— ∞ ————

WE ARE AFRAID OF OUR own responses, our own emotions, our own sensation and our own sexuality because we are trained to be ashamed of our own body, our own feelings, our own sensations and our own sexuality. We have been indoctrinated into the belief that our bodies are sinful, that our feelings are not to be trusted, that our sexuality is sinful and that we must suppress all of these aspects of our being to be good. We are afraid of all of these aspects of our being because we taught to believe we are not okay because we have them.

We are afraid to express ourselves openly, honestly and authentically because we fear being judged for whatever we are experiencing so we hide and suppress everything. From the time we wake up until the time we go to sleep, we live in a state of conflict, tension and anxiety because we are hiding and suppressing what we are experiencing. We are afraid because if we allow our self to feel what we are really feeling, and express what we are really feeling and thinking we will feel shame and embarrassment and be ridiculed and rejected.

Our real responses are always moving in us and through us below the surface of the image we show and social pretenses we have developed to hide them. When we sleep or when we are meditating or alone and in some reverie whatever is moving through us rises to the surface of our awareness. Our suppressed responses come to the surface when we are not lost in our social act, our pretended image that we develop to hide and avoid what is really happening in us.

When we are alone, our real feelings rise and this can bring up fear and anxiety. We are afraid because our feelings and thoughts rise and we are afraid to feel our real feelings and the sensations that come with them. When we are alone our thoughts and feelings come to the surface and we can't fully hide them, suppress them or deny them and they rise to the surface of our awareness in the form of feelings, sensations, images, thoughts, and dreams, with all of the emotional and sensory reactions that are moving in us. The responses we are suppressing are revealed in our dreams, revealing what we are unwilling to see and feel when we are awake.

The only real resolution to this dilemma is to accept ourselves as we really are and get centered in our self and allow ourselves to feel all of it and see all of it. If we are alone we begin to relax into our thoughts, feelings and sensations, into what is really happening in us. As we relax into our actual responses, what we are really feeling, thinking, and sensing is able to flow again.

Then we can begin to see that all of our responses are simply part of being a human being, just the way we are and we can begin to allow our real responses to flow through us more freely. Accepting all of it, allowing all of it, all of our feelings, sensations, thoughts, ideas, images, fantasies, visions, dreams, perceptions, frees us from our patterns of hiding and suppressing and we can begin to be how we really are.

Our feelings, sensations and thoughts are continuously moving through us and the only reason we feel disturbed is because we have been taught to believe these parts of us are bad and shouldn't be happening in us. We have been trained to hide, suppress and reject our self for being the way we are. We are trained to reject and feel bad about our emotions and our sexuality and our enjoyment of sexual pleasure in our penis, our vagina, our clitoris, our nipples and our anus. We were trained to think these parts of us are bad, dirty and sinful and we are taught to feel ashamed of our sexual thoughts, desires and actions, so we suppress and hide our sexuality to maintain an image of non-sexual goodness, so others will accept us and so that we can accept our self.

We are afraid of our desire for sexual pleasure because we were taught that being sexual is bad and that we are bad for wanting and enjoying sex. We are sexual beings, designed by the energy of the Universe to be sexual in spite of all of these socially fabricated beliefs.

We are afraid of our own responses, our own body, our own emotions, our own sensations and our own sexuality because of our socially fabricated ideas that there is something wrong with us. We hide these parts of us and are afraid of showing ourselves to one another because we have been trained to think these parts are unacceptable. We hide our real self and pretend something else, hiding our bodies and suppressing our own responses because we think there is something wrong with us.

We are human beings with a body, mind and emotions that are flowing in us and through us continuously. We respond emotionally, sensuously and mentally and these responses guide us through the experiences of life, bringing us together with what is most resonant with us. We are designed to be emotional and to enjoy sensations of pleasure but we have been oppressed with the belief that there is something wrong with these parts of us. It's no small task to let go of these socially fabricated beliefs and accept ourselves, our body, our feelings, our sensations of pleasure that are moving through us continuously and to freely give expression to these parts of ourselves, openly and honestly in our relationships.

We have learned to be afraid of our own body, feelings, thoughts and sensations and to believe they are bad and will mislead us and get us in trouble if we feel them and follow them. We are afraid of being who and how we really are in fear of being bad, rejected, criticized, ridiculed, judged, ostracized and abused by others.

CHAPTER 14

Our Relationships

——— ∞∞∞ ———

WHEN WE ARE SUPPRESSING OUR real responses, we are hiding our real self from others and preventing them from seeing who we really are and thus, preventing our self from experiencing real intimacy. Suppressing and hiding our real responses is us creating an artificial separation from our self and from one another which causes confusion and disturbances in us and consequently, in our relationships. We all sense when something isn't being expressed, when something is being hidden or denied and we feel the energy of disturbance which interferes with our ability to relate to one another openly or honestly.

When we hide and suppress our real responses we are creating disturbance in our self and this disturbance is felt by everyone and affects all of our relationships. When we suppress our real responses, hiding what is really happening in us, we confuse our self and one another. When we pretend something other than what we are feeling, thinking, sensing we send confused messages because we are feeling one feeling and expressing something different. This creates confusion and disturbance in us and in our relationships because it prevents us from being real and showing our real self to one another. We prevent ourselves from seeing or being seen and prevent ourselves from experiencing real intimacy.

We are afraid to show what we are really feeling in fear that we will be rejected for showing something that is not acceptable to the people around us. We learn these patterns of thought and behavior in our society and we recreate these patterns of suppressing and hiding in all of our relationships. We all say we want intimacy but we prevent it by not being real with one another. We can never experience intimacy while we are suppressing and hiding our real responses from one another. Intimacy is the connection we experience when we allow ourselves to see and be seen. In to me see.

CHAPTER 15

Intimacy

———— ⊗⊗⊗ ————

CREATING INTIMACY IS SOMETHING WE create by showing our real selves to one another. Intimacy happens when we show ourselves openly and honestly to one another, allowing ourselves to see and be seen, as we really are. Intimacy comes from the open, honest and authentic expression of our real responses with one another. We can't create intimacy as long as we suppress and hide our real responses. When we are hiding our real responses, we are preventing our real self from being seen and we are preventing real connection from happening.

When we don't show ourselves to one another or express our real thoughts, feelings and sensations we create relationships built on pretense and our pretended responses can never create intimacy because they aren't real and not the expression of who we really are. Intimate relationships come from the open, honest and authentic expression of our feelings, thoughts and sensations in the moment as we are relating to one another.

The suppression of our real responses prevents us from showing our real self, sharing what is really going on and knowing one another intimately. Hiding and suppressing our real responses prevents us from being real or of having real relationships.

When we first meet we feel turned on to one another, excited and this energy is the energy that brings us together. As we spend more time together, our patterns of hiding, suppressing and pretending take over and we begin hiding our real responses from one another and this creates separation between us. We hide, suppress and present pretended responses we hope will get acceptance and maintain a pleasant relationship but this actually prevents us from being real and creating the very thing we want, which is intimacy.

When we express something other than our real responses, we are hiding and suppressing and we are disconnecting from our real self and therefor from one another. When we do this we feel disconnected and disturbed and we blame one another for the disturbance. We don't realize we are causing our own disconnection and disturbance by hiding and suppressing our real responses.

This is a common pattern of behavior in our relationships. We hide our real responses and keep ourselves separate from ourselves and from the people we love and then we feel the pain of not feeling the closeness we want to feel. We hide our real self and feel the pain of not being seen and think others are causing our pain. We think they are the source of our separateness and consequent hurt, pain, anger and sadness, so we blame one another, thinking the pain we feel is being caused by them. We hide and suppress our own responses and wonder what is wrong, why we aren't happy and why we can't seem to connect and why our relationships aren't intimate the way we want them to be and hoped they would be.

We are creating our relationships from how we see ourselves, how we feel about ourselves and consequently how we relate to one another. If we are hiding and suppressing what we are really feeling and thinking we are creating relationships of pretense, separation, oppression, suppression, control, domination, manipulation, rejection, and conflict and wonder why we live in pain, disturbance, conflict, confusion, unhappiness and relational failure.

Living according to our socially fabricated belief that there is something wrong with us is preventing us from being who we really are and showing who we really are and this prevents us from creating intimate experiences with one another. Our patterns of hiding, suppressing and pretending are covering up our real self and preventing us from being real, being seen and creating intimate relational experiences. When we hide and suppress our real responses, we are hiding from one another and our relationships are disconnected, distant, empty and unfulfilling. This is commonly referred to as "growing apart".

Our beliefs about how we are supposed to be are not real, are in the way of being who we really are and yet they have become what we live in, like a movie in our mind, in which we are performing a role. Our pretenses have replaced our real self and we live in the illusion of what we are pretending. We pretend to be what we are not and lose our connection to our real self and consequently, to our relationship with one another. We are trying to suppress something that can't be fully suppressed, our real self and this is causing all the conflict we are experiencing.

We try to be happy while suppressing our real feelings and no matter what we do to feel okay, nothing we do works because we are not accepting our self, as we really are and we are not showing or expressing our real self as we really are, so no one else can see who we really are.

We get stuck in our patterns of hiding and pretending and don't realize we are suppressing ourselves and keeping our self from being seen. We don't realize that hiding and suppressing our real responses is the source of our disturbance and our inability to connect to our self and one another.

Our society's fabricated beliefs dominate our minds, our reactions, our behaviors, our relationships and our social institutions. We say we want to be free and to live freely but we live in a society that practices oppression, suppression, repression and lives in an illusion about how we should be. We have been trying to live freely while hiding and suppressing our real feelings, sensations and thoughts and "acting out" pretended social roles.

Beliefs are our minds attempt to explain and define life but beliefs are not the reality of who and how we are and they do not represent our actual way of being. When we impose our socially learned beliefs onto reality we interfere with the reality of who we really are, our real responses and our real way of being.

The conflict we feel inside, our arguments with one another, the wars we fight, are all the result of attempting to impose these false social beliefs onto one another. We fight over who is right and who is wrong, we criticize, judge and blame the people we are judging for our judgments. We act out our socially learned beliefs and try to impose our beliefs on one another. We are all so focused on living according to our beliefs about how we should be, we aren't being real with our self or with one another and this is creating all of our conflicts.

Our Universe is perfect, just as it is and we are a perfect part of this perfection and when we accept this, accept our self and others, as we really are, then we can truly be how we are and we will be able to enjoy our self, one another and experience the joy of real intimacy.

CHAPTER 16

Struggle to Be Okay

———⁂———

WE ALL STRUGGLE TO BE okay, according to some belief we have about what it is to be good. We fabricate a role to fit in and be good according to our learned cultural beliefs. We have been taught to believe we are not okay so we struggle to be okay but as long as we believe we are not okay we can never do enough to be okay. We are stuck in a mental conundrum of thinking we are bad and trying to be good, in a world that believes we are bad. Our belief that we are bad prevents us from accepting ourselves and feeling okay with how we are and these beliefs prevent us from seeing that we are the perfection of the universe in human form. We can't resolve this dilemma by hiding and suppressing ourselves and pretending to be some way we are not because we are the way we are created to be and we can't change that and there is nothing wrong with us in the first place. We already are perfect manifestations of the Universe, just the way we are.

CHAPTER 17

Rejection and Acceptance

———— ⌘ ————

WE ARE TRAINED, LIKE PAVLOV'S dog, to salivate to the bell of social acceptance, using positive and negative reinforcement in the form of rejection and acceptance to get us to conform to socially fabricated beliefs. We are rejected when we show something that is considered bad and we are praised when we are following the prevailing social beliefs. Rejection feels painful and acceptance feels good, so we learn quickly to do what we are told. The social strategy is "If you behave according to my dictates you get a positive response. If you behave outside of my dictates you will get a negative response." We get punished or praised for how we behave, according to the prevailing social beliefs about what is good and what is bad.

We are afraid of rejection so we suppress our real responses and pretend to be the way the society around us says we should be. We deny our real way of being in exchange for the acceptance of others.

Suppressing, hiding and pretending are our conditioned responses to our fear of rejection and our desire for acceptance. We want to be loved and accepted, so we do whatever it takes to get it from the people around us. We pretend to think and feel what we are taught to think and feel, in order to avoid rejection and get acceptance. In this way, we have all been conditioned to use rejection and acceptance as a medium of exchange in our relationships with one another. We have learned to manipulate and control one another with acceptance and rejection.

We reject or accept one another as a way of controlling one another. Our relationships have become an experience of suppressing, hiding and pretending to gain acceptance and avoid rejection. We were trained to control ourselves and to be controlled through reward and punishment, acceptance and rejection. We learn to hide and suppress our real self and impose our beliefs and expectations on one another and in the process we settle into a vague sense of disconnection, separation and discomfort and give up on our desire for real intimacy.

In an atmosphere of oppression, suppression, repression, imposition, control, possession and mutual domination, we attempt to create loving relationships and these patterns of mutual hiding, suppressing, pretense, manipulation and control are why we can't create real connection.

We stop enjoying one another because our training to hide, suppress and pretend is preventing us from being who we really are, showing one another who we really are and connecting to one another intimately.

CHAPTER 18

Conditioning

———— ⋙⋘ ————

OUR PARENTS ARE OUR FIRST contact with another human being and we look to them for love, acceptance, connection, our very survival, so they are our first and most important influence. We look to them as our source of security, love, approval and acceptance and they are our first teachers and primary role models. They are who we imitate in energy, voice, facial expressions, how they communicate, how they relate to us and to one another. They set the tone and the patterns of energy, thought and behavior in showing us what is allowed and what is not and reinforcing their way of seeing and responding to life with either, acceptance or rejection.

We learn to suppress whatever stimulates their negative reactions and we learn to show only what gets a positive response in our attempt to get love, acceptance and security. We develop patterns of behavior in childhood that fit into our parents expectations and act them out in all of our relationships with others for the rest of our lives, in our attempt to get love, approval and security.

It is difficult to see our own patterns of thought and behavior because we learn them gradually, like we learn language and it's just how we see things and how we learn to act. We accept how we think and behave as "normal" and we come to believe that we are being who we really are according to these ideas about "how we should be" even though they are not who we really are, not our natural responses to life and this learned pattern of suppressing our natural responses causes conflict in us, with our real self because they do not represent who we really are and consequently we also create conflict with others.

We have been trained to believe there is something wrong with the way we are and that we have to suppress some parts of us to gain love, acceptance and security. We learned ways of thinking and relating, which influence the way we think, the way we see, the way we behave and the way we relate to one another. The problem is that these ways of thinking, seeing and relating are disconnected from who we really are, from our actual responses and are the cause of the conflict we feel and the conflict we create in our relationships.

When we let go of these patterns of seeing, thinking and behaving and just tune into our own responses and accept our self as we really are, we come back into harmony with our real self and in the process we let go of the beliefs that have confined us and limited us, especially the belief that there is something wrong with us. When we let go of the socially fabricated beliefs of our culture, the illusions about how we "should" be disappear like a mirage in the desert. When we accept our self, as we really are, our whole body, mind, emotions, sensations, we relax into who we really are and our whole being relaxes, and we feel a sense of peace and harmony and begin to ease into our real self and into real relationships with one another.

CHAPTER 19

My Personal Version of the Illusion

———— ∞ ————

MY PERSONAL VERSION OF THE social illusion was pretending to be good on the outside and seeing my self as bad on the inside. I pretended to be good but felt bad; frustrated, angry, hostile, scarred, resentful, rejecting and judgmental on the inside. I was very sexual but pretended to be calm, cool and collected on the outside. I lived in my own version of the social illusion, pretending to be one way and feeling different on the inside. I never understood why I felt so uncomfortable with my self, why my relationships didn't work and why they would begin with such mutual excitement, enjoyment and pleasure and eventually turn into conflict. Excitement, passion and appreciation drowned in the flood of negativity, criticism and judgement based in the socially fabricated belief that I was bad and wrong for being the way I am.

In an atmosphere of mutual self rejection, our relationship would become mutual criticism, judgement, blame, argument, aggression and hostility. Over time our negative patterns of blame, criticism and judgement took over and we became focused on what we didn't like or accept about our self and one another. We tried to be loving but our conditioning to criticize, judge and reject got stimulated and our patterns of reactive behavior took over. We wanted to be accepting but our belief that their was something wrong with us and our patterns of suppression and rejecting self and one another got triggered and dominated our interactions.

Love, joy, happiness, and pleasure turned into conflict when we didn't accept our self or one another. We try to be loving and create relationships of love, acceptance and positive experiences but our conditioning to think there is something wrong takes over and we reject our self and one another, rather than loving and accepting one another. We don't want to be negative but we have patterns of self rejection, oppression, suppression, control and imposition and we have a hard time letting go of them and changing our patterns to love and acceptance.

We don't like being judged and criticized but we are all trained to judge and criticize our self, our partners, our kids, our friends, our family and everyone else. Judgment, criticism and rejection is part of our socially conditioned thinking and behavior that we learned and developed in growing up in our society.

We have difficulty changing these thoughts and behaviors because they are unconscious patterns of thought, belief, attitude and behavior. Our conditioning to criticize, judge and reject is so embedded in our thinking, our reactions and our way of relating, so we don't realize we are doing it. We don't realize our patterns of negativity have taken over in us and are so ingrained and unconscious that they are causing us to relate the way we do and are interfering with our positive feelings of excitement, love and appreciation.

We are trained to think there is something wrong with us so we don't realize our patterns of negative thought, reaction and behavior is what is causing all the conflict we are experiencing.

We or move specifically our thinking is the source of the conflicts we are experiencing in our self and in our relationships but we don't realize it because we are so mesmerized by our own patterns of thought, reaction and behavior. We haven't been able to see this because we are trained to believe there is something wrong with us and we are lost in this pattern of belief, thought and behavior.

We try resolving our issues by talking about them, what we see as our problems and how we can resolve them but this conversation comes out of the idea that there is something wrong with us, so our attempts at resolution get us more deeply embedded in our socially learned beliefs about what is wrong with one of us. We criticize, judge, blame, reject, resist, push and try to figure out what is wrong with us or them and try to change our self and them, in an attempt to resolve the conflict but our discussions about what is wrong with us takes us deeper into our patterns of negativity and rejection.

We react to one another with hurt and anger while we continue in our pattern of criticizing, judging and rejecting. We feel hurt and angry when someone rejects us and yet, we can't seem to stop from doing the same thing. We don't see that our belief that there is something wrong with us is causing the negative experiences that we are having. We actually believe there is something wrong with one of us.

This is why our relationships aren't working and can't work. We play out our learned patterns of thinking there is something wrong with us, while blaming, criticizing, judging and rejecting one another and wonder why we can't seem to create mutually loving relationships.

We all want to be loved and accepted for who we are and yet we are stuck in our conditioned patterns of rejection based on the socially fabricated belief that there is something wrong with us. How can we connect and experience love or intimacy if we don't accept ourselves and one another and actually show ourselves as we really are to one another openly and honestly.

We suppress and hide ourselves in fear that someone will see the things we are trying to hide and suppress and therefor we live in patterns of thought and behavior that can never be resolved by talking about our problems. As long as we are living in socially fabricated patterns of thinking that there is something wrong with us for being the way we are, emotional or sexual or just different we cannot resolve the conflicts we are experiencing in our self or with one another.

CHAPTER 20

Accepting Our Real Self

———— ✺ ————

WHEN I FINALLY FACED MY self, my real feelings, thoughts and sensations, I began to see that all of my conflict, all of my upsets were being caused by my own thinking and that I was the source of my thinking, my energy and that I was source of the conflict that I was creating with others. I didn't want to see this. I tried to avoid seeing this but I saw that my beliefs and my thinking was causing my negative energy and experiences with others.

I didn't accept my self or anyone else and was therefor in conflict with my self and everyone. I had developed a pattern of belief that no one was okay, including me, thinking there was something wrong with me and everyone else, a pattern I learned in growing up in my society that was creating my way of being, thinking and relating and therefor creating my experience of reality

My father had these patterns of his society of self rejection, disconnection from his true self and was in conflict with himself and with others and he passed it on to me, just as he passed on language. He was hurt, angry, hostile and had become negatively focused, like his father. He had become like his father and he passed it all on to me, "sins of the father". We learned to avoid his anger by hiding and suppressing ourselves when he was around but we also learned his patterns of negativity. We suppressed anything that might disturb him or stimulate a negative reaction in him but we were also learning his language of negativity. We were being trained by his energy and behavior to hide and suppress ourselves and we were receiving the transmission of "the social way and belief" that no one was okay and must be oppressed and suppressed.

As I moved out into the rest of the world, I found this same kind of negative and oppressive energy in school, the army, the church, the police and the institutions of our society. In response to this we either submit or rebel, but one way of another we learn fit ourselves into the society and the socially fabricated beliefs of our society and we each develop our own ways of coping and dealing with the oppression of our society.

Sigmund Freud said "Since the beginning of civilization mankind has had but one choice; to conform or not to conform. Should he choose to conform his life is over for every decisions he makes from cradle to grave will be determined by society-at-large. If he chooses not to conform, he buys himself one more choice; to be become outlaw or hero."

I think we have another choice and that is to simply be who we really are, present with our own way of being and our own actual responses to life and in so doing leave the socially fabricated illusion.

We learn to hide, suppress and alter our real self in order to fit into our society. Our patterns of thought and behavior are based in a set of socially fabricated beliefs that aren't real. If we stay in this socially fabricated illusion we develop our particular role in our societies fabricated beliefs. Our way of being and relating is determined by our beliefs and is based on the role we have chosen to play, based on our role models and our particular way of fitting in to the world of people around us.

Our patterns of hiding and suppressing are the cause of all of our internal conflict, our dysfunctional patterns of mind and body and the cause of our inability to be how we really are and to relate authentically with one another or create truly intimate and functional relationships that are real and connected.

Our society passes on these false beliefs and dysfunctional patterns to us just like they pass on language, through modeling and imitation. Our parents pass on what had been passed to them, "sins of the father". They were human beings living in a world of illusion, a world that didn't accept them or support them in being who and how they really are and they passed on these patterns of thought and behavior to us. They were oppressed and trained to hide and suppress their true being and were therefor in conflict who they really were and consequently with the world in which they lived and they passed this view and behavior on to us.

They were part of a society that had been indoctrinated and conditioned into the socially fabricated belief that there was something wrong with them and they passed these beliefs and ways on to us. They were taught to think there was something wrong with their emotions, their sexuality and their unique and individual way of being and to reject their true selves and to live within the limiting beliefs of their society. They were human beings living in a world of illusion.

We all learn to believe in the socially fabricated view of right/wrong. This is our training, our conditioning and our indoctrinated view of reality. We learn these ways of seeing and behaving and we think we are being real and living life the way we are supposed to when in fact, we are performing a socially indoctrinated performance. We don't know we are suppressing and denying our actual responses or that our whole way of seeing life is the result of a learned socially fabricated belief that isn't real or true.

Our beliefs are a socially fabricated conceptual view of reality, a mental movie, a learned idea that is stimulating our way of seeing and relating to our self and our world, our reactions, our behavior and our interactions with one another. As long as we continue to believe in these socially fabricated illusions we will continue to create conflicts in our self and in our relationships.

CHAPTER 21

The Illusion of Sin

———◦◦◦———

THE ILLUSION OF SIN IS based in the idea that there is something wrong with us. The original meaning of the word sin was "to miss the mark", or to misunderstand. We have been taught to believe that we are born into sin because our ancestors violated a commandment from God and that we are born into sin by birth and inheritance because of the actions of these two individuals. We are told that because they violated God's commandment that they had to hide their bodies and were "cast out of paradise" forever. This story is the basis of the false belief that there is something wrong with us and this one belief controls the minds and thinking of most of us.

This story was created by human beings trying to control other human beings and is really about oppression and teaching us to control ourselves by hiding and suppressing our own natural way of being and this one false belief is in the way of us realizing and accepting ourselves as we truly are and that we are perfect exactly the way we are.

We are told we have to hide our bodies, suppress our emotions and our sexuality and feel guilty and ashamed of ourselves for being human, because Adam and Eve "ate from the tree of the knowledge of good and evil". What does this really mean? I think it means that they started thinking and this separated them from nature, from their natural way of being and therefor from paradise or nature.

This one false perception, this sin, this misunderstanding, this teaching has caused us to hide and suppress ourselves as we really are and to hide from one another, our natural way of being human.

We are told that our sexuality is sinful and that we are sinful because we want, desire and enjoy sexual pleasure. We are taught to believe that our very desire for sexual pleasure is a sin and that we have to suppress it, deny it and abstain from sexual expression unless it is sanctioned by the religious leaders and society.

These teachings come from human beings trying to control other human beings, who say they got this teaching from God, in order to give these beliefs credibility but these are just beliefs, made up by human beings who were trying to control one another.

These beliefs are illusions but they have been part of our cultural belief system for so long, they are embedded in our thinking, our reactions and our behavior. Most of us believe these illusions about life, God, sex and emotions, because we were indoctrinated into them from birth and they are part of our cultural view of reality.

We use words like God, Allah, Jehova, Krishna, Elokim, Yahwea, Great Spirit, Shiva, Kali, Chita and many others to refer to the energy of the Universe, out of which the material world emanates. We are the ones making up the words we use to refer to this energy. Scientists call the invisible force of the Universe wave and the physical part, particle or mass.

The physical world is the material expression of this energy, which is life, which is creation, which is nature, which is the Universe and this includes us. Beliefs about creation came from human beings trying to explain the universe and trying to get everyone to believe the same way so they could control the thinking and behavior of other human beings in their social group.

In the absence of real understanding they made up stories to explain, understand and influence this energy in their favor, praying in the hope that prayers will bring rain, a good harvest, the cure of an illness or whatever outcome was desired.

In place of true understanding, we make up beliefs about supernatural beings and pray to them in hopes they will give us what we need. We make up stories about God making us leave paradise/nature but it was really us, who made up the stories to explain existence so we could feel more secure.

We are born with a fully functioning neurobiological system that includes sensations, feelings and thoughts that are there to guide us and provide us with the ability to respond and live life successfully. We have feelings, sensations, thoughts, visions and fantasies that guide us if we follow them. but we have been taught to reject our own responses in favor of an idea about God, a being separate from us to whom we attribute the power that we ourselves have because we are this energy in human form.

Beliefs come from human beings trying to explain and control life, so we can feel safe, secure, and get what we need to survive. Beliefs come from us and not from God. God is just one of the words we make up to refer to the universe so we can give ourselves a sense of security about life.

We use many different words to describe the energy of the Universe, like Great Spirit, Tao, Buddha, Christ, Yahway, Elokim, Allah, God, Jehovah, Krishna, Shiva, Abraxes, Zeus, Kali, Chita, Goddess and these are all just words made up by human beings to refer to the energy of the Universe.

We make up stories to explain the Universe to ourselves and we pass our stories on to our offspring. We make up stories to explain reality and think our explanation is reality. Reality is the way everything already is, nature, as it is, us as we really are and our beliefs about life, are just our made up conceptual ideas and explanations about it.

We have been trying to understand and explain the Universe since the beginning of human existence. We once believed that God was nature and that by praying to that form of God, the water God, the Sun God, the Moon God, the rain God, we could influence this aspect of God to give us what we needed. Our beliefs formed out of our needs, our fears, our wants, our desires and our perception of the world. We saw the different forms of nature as God and developed our beliefs about how to appease this energy and gain what we needed.

We were trying to control the forces of the Universe through prayer and behaviors meant to appease this energy, this being and get what we needed to survive and prosper. We have refined our beliefs as we have evolved in knowledge and awareness but our beliefs come from us and not from this energy of the Universe that we call God. Our beliefs are our mind's perception of reality that we believe and follow in our attempt to align ourselves with this energy, in order to survive.

We are how we are, how we were designed to be but we are still the way the universe is manifesting in human form and we are living in socially fabricated beliefs about "how we should be" that is not real but fits into the stories our ancestors made up about the Universe.

We are the energy of the Universe in human form. We have all been conditioned to believe these stories that attempt to explain a Universe that our ancestors didn't understand and we continue to hold onto these ancient perceptions about reality because we were indoctrinated into them and we are afraid to let them go and accept reality as it is.

We have evolved in our understanding of how the Universe really works in many ways but we still hold on to these ancient beliefs, in spite of our new understanding. We have evolved in our understanding beyond previous generations and our children will evolve beyond ours but this requires letting go of the false beliefs into which we have been reared. Reality is simply what is and as we are able to see this clearly we also see the way the Universe really is and our ideas about it must also evolve.

We are human beings, with sensations, feelings, thoughts and perceptions that are our neurobiological system, guiding us through life. Accepting our feelings, sensations and body the way it is, with all of it's parts and functions gives us access to the neurobiological system that guides us through life. Accepting ourselves as we are, with all of our body parts, all of our feelings, sensations, thoughts and images that are flowing through us, allows us access to our natural biological system and allows it to function fully, as it was designed to function.

When we accept our self, as we really are, including our sexuality, our emotions, our mind and our body, we can see the perfection of our own being and we can allow ourselves to be what we already are, human beings, living in a world of illusion.

We experience sexual sensations and all of these sensations are part of our natural way of being, the way we were created to be and they are there to encourage us to be sexual so that we will come together in positive, loving interactions and reproduce.

This is the reality of being human, this is how we are created to be, how we are designed to be and how we are manifesting to be in human form by the design of the energy of the Universe.

CHAPTER 22

Living in the Illusion

———— ∞∞∞ ————

WE LIVE IN A SOCIALLY fabricated illusion about how we are supposed to be, that does not match how we really and we have been trained to think the illusion is real so we are uncomfortable with how we really are. We hold onto these socially fabricated beliefs, as if they are real and we are trained to think these beliefs are better than the reality of how we really are. We are afraid of letting go of these beliefs because we have been trained to believe that we will be punished by God if we don't adhere to them and we are also afraid of being rejected, abused and ostracized by our society.

Leaders of religions, governments and other social groups have used these false beliefs to control us and do not want individuals really being free and following their own inner responses so they perpetuate these beliefs as if they are real. Consequently, leaders of religions and governments see individuals as subservient to the group and it's beliefs.

The suppression of our individual responses is a sin against humanity, against us, against who we really are, against nature and against creation it self and are incredibly detrimental to our health and well being. These false, socially fabricated beliefs are interfering with our connection with our real self, our connection to our own responses and to our authentic expression of our responses, our ability to tune into them, guide our own life and they are interfering with our ability to relate authentically to one another.

This is why it is so important for each of us to center in our self, into our own experience, into our own responses and allow them to guide us toward what is right for us, amidst all the social pressure to conform to the prevailing social beliefs. We live in a socially fabricated illusion about how we should be and we either tune into our own responses and follow them or we continue following the conceptual illusions of our society.

CHAPTER 23

How To Know We Are In The Illusion

— ⌘ —

WE ARE IN THE ILLUSION when we feel bad about our self, when we think there is something wrong with us or think we should be different than we are or when we are hiding or suppressing our real responses and not accepting our self or reality, as it is.

When we feel disturbed with some aspect of our humanness and are judging, criticizing, blaming, arguing, correcting, intimidating, tyrannizing, dominating, oppressing, suppressing and trying to control some part of reality, we are living in the social illusion about how someone or something should be and not accepting that aspect of reality. When we are arguing inside our own mind, we are in the social illusion and our indoctrinated conceptual mind is arguing with reality and trying to impose our beliefs about reality, onto reality, as it really is. As Byron Katie has said, "if you argue with reality you lose, but only %100 of the time."

The belief that we shouldn't be angry, sad, scarred, in love, naked or sexual is part of this socially fabricated illusion into which we were all born and indoctrinated. The belief that we shouldn't express our feelings or thoughts openly, honestly or authentically is part of the conceptual illusion into which we were all indoctrinated.

We have been taught to believe we shouldn't express our self, openly, honestly, and passionately. We have been taught to reject reality so completely, that we think some part of us is bad and should be hidden and suppressed. When we are living and operating within our socially fabricated conceptual beliefs about reality, we are in the social illusion. The beliefs about how we should be are the conceptual illusions of our society and when we are living in them as if they are real, we are living in the social illusion and denying who we really are.

CHAPTER 24

Mass Illusion

———— ⚬⚬⚬ ————

WE LIVE IN A MASS social illusion. Our whole society is living in an illusion about reality that isn't real. This illusion is the perpetuation of an ancient false perception of reality. I call them illusions because they are only a conceptual view of reality, an idea that has been taught to us as real and so it seems real, but is not. Like a mirage in the desert, a reflection of light off the sand that appears to be water, when you see them clearly you can see that they are just illusions. The illusion seems real because we were raised with it and it seems real and it isn't easy to see that it is just an idea, an illusion of thought that isn't based in reality.

We are social beings and we are dependent on our group for our sense of security and survival, so we are terrified of letting go of these beliefs and seeing things differently than our social group. We have learned to fit into our group by conforming to the group's beliefs and we are afraid of letting go of these beliefs and depending on our own responses and our own inner guidance to survive. We are terrified that we might not be able to survive without the group's support, approval and acceptance, so we cling to the beliefs of our group.

We are driven by our need to fit in and to feel secure. We are very invested in maintaining the social illusion because we think we have to maintain our role in the illusion to maintain our role in the group and thus our sense of belonging and feeling secure. Our drive to belong and fit into the group drives us to maintain the social illusions, even when our own experience is different and does not fit into the social illusion. We try to maintain the pretense of being the way the social illusions say we should be, just to maintain our relationship within our group. Our drive to fit in is so strong we suppress our own responses and pretend the learned social responses to fit in to some version of the group illusion, just to assure our place in the group.

We each develop our own personal version of the social beliefs in our own mind, so we can fit in and be part of our group. We develop our role and we refine our role, as we learn, first in our families and then in the larger society, to fit into our group's view of reality.

Our families are our primary group and source of security, so we try hard to develop our place in our family. As we move out into the larger world we refine our role to fit into the larger social group and it's beliefs. We are driven to fit in by our need and desire for security which depends on being accepted and approved of by our group. We feel fear and anxiety in being independent, unique or different from our group, so we learn to pretend to be like we are told we should be and in the process we deny our own experience, just to fit in. Our fear of being rejected compels us to maintain our role in the group because we think we won't survive without the acceptance and approval of our group, so we pretend, even when our own personal experience of reality does not fit into our group's view. Even when we are aware of our own unique way of being, we negate our own experience of reality to fit into our group. This is truly, gaining the world and losing our self.

Allowing our self to feel and express our real feelings is threatening for us after a lifetime of hiding, suppressing and pretending. Occasionally, we may feel like we are in the flow of our own experience and even allow our self to feel our real responses but much of the time we are maintaining our image and our role within the social matrix. We learn to suppress, hide, pretend, criticize and judge our self if we are feeling something that is unacceptable to this social view of reality. We are intimidated by the possibility that others will see us as different from our social group and it's beliefs about reality.

We play our role for so long that it becomes unconscious and automatic and we are unaware that we are playing a role. We reinforce one another's roles and maintain the social game and common social illusions. We notice the pretensions of others and criticize them for being pretentious but for the most part, we are unaware that we are also playing our pretentious role in the socially fabricated illusion of "how we should be".

The idea that the entire world is involved in an illusion may be hard to accept at first because we have come to believe that this fabricated view of reality is real. We want to hold onto our place in our group, so we hold onto the social illusions and our pretense and believe that we are being real. In order to maintain our place in the group, we suppress our real responses and show only what is acceptable to our group.

We are all playing in a social movie of "how we are pretending to be" in order to fit into the social illusion of "how we are supposed to be". Facing our own pretense and illusions can be intimidating to us because we think our socially fabricated view of reality, is reality and we are afraid to see that it isn't and feel and express our real responses and face the possible rejection by our group. We might be rejected, excommunicated, abused, ostracized and shunned by group and lose the security we feel in playing our role in the group.

We learned these beliefs about "how we should be" and have lost our ability to be who we really are and simply be present with and accept the way we really are. We live in these beliefs, behave according to these beliefs, pay homage to these beliefs, maintain these beliefs and perpetuate these beliefs. Our beliefs are so deeply embedded in our thinking, our feelings, our sensations, our behaviors, our postures, our attitudes, our language, our bodies and the way our minds perceive reality, that we have lost our connection to the reality of what is really going on inside our self. We are conditioned to believe in the social beliefs so completely that we are dissociated from our real responses and are unable to see and feel our responses, as they really are or to express them openly and honestly.

We live in and perpetuate these conceptual illusions, while we suppress the reality of our own inner experience. Our own inner experience is the only reality we can ever really experience and yet we deny it, in order to fit in to our group and it's conceptual beliefs about reality. Our beliefs about reality are interfering with our direct experience of reality and this is causing the conflict we feel.

Our mental, emotional and physical dysfunctions, as well as the conflicts we are experiencing in our relationships are the result of our disconnection from our own responses. We are trained and conditioned from birth to live in these illusions and wonder why we are so uncomfortable with our self and in conflict with one another. As long as we live in our illusions about "how we should be" we will be in conflict with our real self and we will consequently be in conflict with one another.

Our beliefs effect us in profound ways because they dominate our thinking, our perception of reality and our reactions to reality. Because of our beliefs we reject our self and we reject others. We criticize, judge and reject our self and one another and live in a state of conflict and negative energy. We are mean to one another because we believe in the illusions of our society so completely, we even kill one another to impose our beliefs on one another in our attempt to "force one another to be the way we believe we should be".

We think our beliefs are real and right so we use the power of government, schools, religions, media, police and armies to intimidate everyone into following these fabricated social beliefs. How we really are as human beings is rejected and social beliefs are imposed on all of us. No one is allowed to be the way they really are or to express their authentic responses openly and freely without the threat of some form of rejection.

Throughout the history of human society we have abused one another in many ways to impose the prevailing social beliefs on everyone. We have put one another in stocks, dunked, burned, hanged, water boarded, stoned, shunned, ostracized, exiled and killed one another to impose social beliefs on one another.

The U. S. Congress went into special session when Janis Jackson showed her nipple on national television in a performance at the Super Bowl. Our congress used its power of office to threaten, intimidate and abuse her and the television producers, in order to impose their belief that showing her nipple is bad, wrong and sinful.

We are all indoctrinated into thinking our bodies are sinful and that it is wrong to show our bodies, so we go along with this kind of oppression by our own government, even though it violates our inalienable right to be free and to be how we really are, as we are "endowed by our creator" to be, as our primary social agreement, our constitution has established and guarantees.

Imposing beliefs on one another is tyranny, a rejection of reality, a rejection of our natural way of being and a rejection of life. Janet was rejected for showing a part of her body that is a natural, god given part of us. She was really being stoned in the biblical sense by our congress for not going along with the false social belief that there is something wrong with our bodies. Men show their nipples on national television but women are not allowed to show their nipples, even though this is a clear violation of equal rights and obvious sexual discrimination by our own government but we go along with it because it fits into the false belief that showing our bodies is sinful.

Our constitution prohibits all forms of sexual discrimination, so the U. S. Congress is guilty of violating the Constitution by violating the "inalienable rights" of this individual but we go along with these violations because of our indoctrination into these false social beliefs. Our social institutions impose these beliefs on us because the individuals in office have been indoctrinated into these same false beliefs and think they are doing what is right.

We are all trained to reject our real self, our natural self and to adhere to these socially fabricated beliefs of our group. We are attacked and punished if we don't go along with the social illusions, just as Janet Jackson was abused. Janet didn't violate the law but our Congress did. Janet simply did something that goes against the false belief of our society that our body is sinful and must be covered. We all have nipples by the design of the Universe but if you are a woman, no one is allowed to see them publicly. We don't allow women's nipples to be seen because we have been taught to believe that they are sexual and that the sexual parts of our bodies are sinful and bad.

These socially fabricated beliefs about life are being imposed on us, in an attempt to suppress and control our natural way of being in order to fit into the false beliefs about reality that we inherited from our ancestors. These socially fabricated beliefs are believed by most of us, so we go along with the oppression, abuse and tyranny of our leaders and much of the time, we play a part in the tyranny.

Our sexuality is a natural part of being human and is the most suppressed energy in all of human society. We are taught to believe that our sexual energy is bad and that we must control our sexual energy, hide our sexual energy, suppress our sexual energy, reject our sexual energy, fear our sexual energy and punish anyone who expresses sexual energy.

Women are especially abused for showing their bodies and for being sexual. We are jailed for being naked and for being sexual because of these ancient and false beliefs that teach that these parts of us are bad, wrong and sinful.

We are told that Adam and Eve ate "from the tree of the knowledge of good and evil" after being told not to by God and then felt shame for being naked, so they covered themselves and were cast out of the Garden of Eden and because of this we are all inheritors of this original sin. This story, like all stories, was made up by human beings who attributed it to God, in order to give it credibility, so they could indoctrinate everyone into suppressing and hiding their own natural way of being. These stories have been handed down from generation to generation, as if they are true, and we have been trained to believe they are true. With this kind of story we have been taught to be ashamed of our bodies, our sexuality, our emotions and our natural God given way of being.

We have all been cast out of the Garden of Eden, not by God but by human beings rejecting the way we really are, the way we were created to be and thus we human beings have cast ourselves out of Paradise/nature, by rejecting ourselves, by rejecting what is natural about us and what is natural about life. We have cast ourselves out of paradise and made up a story that God did it to us because we were bad.

Our beliefs don't come from God but from us, human beings wanting to control the behavior of other human beings by convincing us that some part of us is bad. Through these stories and false views of reality, we are trained to suppress and hide parts of us, in order to follow these false beliefs about life.

The imposition of socially fabricated beliefs is about human beings attempting to control other human beings. We are told stories about God rejecting our ancestors and kicking them out of paradise for being naked and sexual, in order to train us to believe being naked and sexual is bad and wrong, so we would hide and suppress what is natural and real about us. The oppression and suppression of our natural way of being is the real sin against life, against nature and against ourselves.

We are afraid of being naked or sexual because we have been taught to believe this is bad and we have been abused for being naked and sexual, the way we naturally are. We were trained to believe that our body, our emotions and our sexuality are bad and sinful and these socially fabricated beliefs are in the way of us accepting our real self, as we really are. These socially fabricated beliefs are in the way of us being fully functional or from expressing ourselves openly, honestly and freely. We have learned to hide and suppress ourselves to fit into these false social beliefs so we play our role in the illusion and pretend to be the way everyone else is pretending to be and in the process we lose touch with who and how we really are.

We believe these beliefs are real, so we suppress our true self, in homage to the illusions we have been taught to believe in. We have been taught to believe that the suppression of our natural way of being is good, moral, godly, right, modest, decent, and civilized but the suppression of our real way of being is a horrible denial of who we are and the real sin against us and a rejection of life.

A belief is just an idea that we think is real, a movie in our mind about life and not the reality of life, as it is. This socially fabricated movie in our mind, like a mirage, seems real but disappears when we get close to it and see that it's only an illusion.

Only when we see that our beliefs are nothing more than ideas about life and realize that they are not real and do not represent the way we really are, can we stop living in this illusion and be how we really are.

Our bodies, our emotional responses and our sexual responses, are all perfect parts of us, just as they are designed to be, by the Universe. We are simply lost in a false social belief about how we should be that isn't real. In seeing that our beliefs are just conceptual illusions we can let them go of them and be how we really are. Accepting our self as we really are is the only way out of the illusion in which we have all been indoctrinated and in which we all live.

CHAPTER 25

The Illusion of How We Should Be

———— ∞ ————

THE BELIEFS ABOUT "HOW WE should be" are the "Greatest Illusion Ever Told" pretending to be honorable and holy. It is not honorable or holy to deny how we really are, to deny life as it is and impose false socially fabricated beliefs on one another. Beliefs are nothing more than ideas we learn and repeat, mental pictures, illusions about reality. They are not good or healthy or holy or real even though we have been taught to believe that they are holy. The oppression and suppression of our natural way of being is not holy or good and imposing these socially fabricated beliefs on anyone is nothing more than tyranny.

When we hide and suppress our self, we are participating in the socially fabricated illusion and perpetuating this illusion and system of control. We may pretend that these beliefs are good and give one another rewards and awards when we follow these beliefs and successfully suppress our natural responses, according to the beliefs but we are participating in an insidious process that is denying our true self and denying ourselves the full life that we could be living.

If we hide and suppress ourselves and pretend to be some way we are not we give up who we really are. This is a denial of how we really are and how we were created to be, in homage to these socially fabricated false beliefs. We pay homage to these socially fabricated beliefs and learn to suppress our self and oppress others and think we are being holy, while we deny the very energy and form that makes us uniquely who we are, as human beings. It seems strange and incredible that we would all buy into this illusion but most of us do and are willing to defend these beliefs to our death.

The freedom to be who we really are, to express our self fully and relate to one another openly, honestly and freely is our inalienable right to "life, liberty and the pursuit of happiness". We are life happening, we are human beings happening and we are endowed by our creator with the inalienable right to be who we are and to express ourselves fully and freely. We are as perfect and natural as the sun and moon. We are human beings and we are sexual and emotional and it is essential to our health and well being to accept all aspects of our being and to give expression to all aspects of our being, fully and freely.

CHAPTER 26

The Oppression of Beliefs

———— ⊲⊳⊳ ————

WE ARE LIVING IN THE oppression of socially fabricated beliefs and we have been indoctrinated into the belief that there is something wrong with us even though there isn't. If I can convince you that there is something wrong with you and teach you to hide, suppress and deny your self and to follow my belief about how you should be then you give me control over you. This is what the spiritual teacher Da Free John called the "Dreaded Gombu or The Imaginary Illness That Religion Seeks To Cure". First someone made up the belief that there was something wrong with us, then convinced everyone that there was and that is how they controlled everyone.

If I can convince you that you are flawed and that you will only be redeemed and forgiven, by following my rules, then I have control over you. If I can convince you that you must hide and suppress your self to be saved, then you will hide and suppress your self and you will train your children to do the same and then I can control you and your children.

We are taught to believe that suppressing our real self, our natural way of being is good and necessary to be saved from our own natural humanness. The belief that we are bad or sinful is an illusion and is a rejection of how we are and how we are created to be. Our cultural beliefs are a form of oppression being imposed on us. Our cultural beliefs set up a conflict in us between how we really are and how we are pretending to be to fit into the false beliefs of our culture. This process of oppression is accomplished through reward and punishment and rejection for being naked, sexual or emotionally expressive. We react with shame and embarrassment in seeing a naked body, feeling sexual energy or feeling our emotional responses because we have been trained to believe these aspects of our being are bad, sinful and unacceptable.

We are taught not to cry, scream, laugh, speak, make noise, be naked, be sexual, touch our self or one another sexually or express our emotions freely. We have been trained to hide and suppress ourselves in homage to these false beliefs and we learn to reject our real self in exchange for a socially created image of propriety. It is like trading in a solid gold coin, our true self, for a counterfeit coin, the social image of goodness. Our social image is not real but it is the social game being played by almost everyone in our society

We have all been indoctrinated and conditioned into believing these socially fabricated beliefs so there is almost unanimous agreement that they are real. We don't question these beliefs because most of us think they are real, even though our own experience does not fit into them. We have been taught to believe our natural way of being is bad and to pretend some socially acceptable way of being. We play a role with one another because we are trained to play these roles. When we suppress our sexual energy or our emotional energy, we are suppressing the very energy that is part of who and how we are designed to be. Sex is a natural aspect of being human and we are meant to be sexual and to pleasure one another sexually. When we allow ourselves to be how we really are and allow our natural energy to flow and express fully and freely, we fulfill ourselves, one another and our natural expression of life, which is what we are.

CHAPTER 27

Creating Conflict

———⊱⊰———

WE CREATE OUR OWN CONFLICT when we hide and suppress our real responses. When we hide and suppress our real responses we are not accepting ourselves the way we really are and we are causing the conflict we feel.

All of our conflict is caused by us not accepting some part of us as we really are and when we do not accept some aspect of our self or others, we are in conflict with that part of us and creating conflict with that aspect of reality. When we do not accept ourselves or others, we feel conflict in our mind, body and emotions. When we do not accept others we experience our non acceptance as conflict with them. When others do not fit into our beliefs about how we think they should be, we are in conflict with how they really are and we reject them because they do not fit into our mental pictures. All conflict is the result of not accepting some aspect of reality and trying to impose our idea of "how we should be" onto the reality of how we really are. When we argue and blame one another for not fulfilling our idea about how the other should be, we are trying to impose our ideas on them and we are rejecting them and reality, as it is.

We think. "If you really loved me, you would be the way I think you should be." The truth is if we really loved them we would accept and honor them the way they really are and when we judge and reject, it is we who are not being accepting or loving. We reject the reality of how the other person is and think they are the problem and that they are wrong because they don't fit into our idea about how they should be. We think our ideas about them are right and the reality of who they are is wrong.

In retaliation for our expectations not being met, we withhold love and acceptance from them to punish them for not being the way we think they should be and for not doing what we want them to do to fulfill our unrealistic expectations. We think the problem is with them, what is wrong with them and we don't see that the problem is us not accepting them. We don't realize that the problem is us not accepting us or them or some aspect of them, some aspect that we don't accept in our self either. We try to impose our beliefs on others, as if they should fulfill our idea about how they should be, and this is some very twisted thinking.

We think our socially fabricated beliefs are right, so we blame them for not fitting into our limiting ideas about how they should be. We blame others for not seeing things our way and for not adhering to our beliefs about "how they should be" and when we are lost in our illusion and think we are right it doesn't matter to us how they really are or what they are really feeling, thinking or experiencing because we think we know what is right and what is wrong about how they should be.

We argue with reality and think our belief about reality is right and reality is wrong. We think our beliefs are more important then the reality of how we really are we wonder why we are in such conflict in our self and with one another while we reject how we really are. Byron Katie said, "when you argue with reality, you lose, but only 100% of the time". We are arguing with reality and we are creating our own conflict through trying to impose our false beliefs on our self and others, as we really are.

Reality does not conform to our beliefs, even if we think that our belief is good and right. Our beliefs are conceptual ideas about reality. When we blame one another, criticize one another, judge one another, impose on one another, reject one another, find fault with one another and oppress one another, we are causing the conflict because we are not accepting reality, as it is. Our beliefs are not reality and do not change the reality of how we really are. It is our socially fabricated beliefs that are in the way of us accepting ourselves and the cause of our conflict and they are interfering with us being the way we really are.

We tyrannize one another with our beliefs because we think our beliefs are right. We try to impose our beliefs on one another, even though our imposition creates conflict in us and in our relationships and even though our beliefs limit us and do not support us in being fully alive, healthy and functional. Werner Erhard said, "do you want to be right or do you want to be happy". We've been choosing to be right over being happy because we do not accept ourselves as we really are.

Our patterns of oppression, suppression, control, rejection and imposition are causing all of the conflict we are feeling and all of the conflict we are creating in our relationships. Happiness and fulfillment can't come from rejection of our self or one another and the imposition of our beliefs on our self or one another. Happiness can only come from the acceptance of our self and others, as we really are.

When we tune into our natural way of being and accept ourselves as we really are, everything we are experiencing will be okay and all of our relationships will unfold naturally from the energy of mutual acceptance.

CHAPTER 28

Control

———— ⊸∞⊷ ————

CONTROL IS BEHIND ALL SOCIALLY fabricated beliefs. Parents try to control their children and religions and governments try to control everyone through reward and punishment. If I can convince you that parts of you are bad, and I can get you to control your self, even when I am not with you then you will suppress your own responses and inhibit your own behavior according to the ideas I have instilled in you. This is what we call brainwashing, indoctrination and conditioning.

Control is the motivation behind all oppression and suppression. Getting us to control our feelings, our thoughts, our sensations and our sexuality is the most common form of social control. We are trained to control our sexual responses and inhibit our sexual behavior by teaching us to believe that sex is bad and that we must control our sexual responses to be good. We are trained from birth to hide our genitals and suppress our sexual responses by shaming us for being naked or sexual.

We are trained to suppress our feelings in exactly the same way. If we express anything openly we are criticized to train us to control our self. We grow up in this socially fabricated atmosphere of oppression to train us to hide and suppress ourselves.

We are trained to hide and suppress what we feel, think, sense and want. We learn to do what others expect of us and we lose our ability to feel what we are really feeling, thinking and sensing.

Our parents, teachers, preachers, police, and politicians teach us to control ourselves in allegiance to these socially fabricated beliefs about how we should be. "I pledge allegiance" is just another part of our indoctrination into giving our power to the socially fabricated beliefs.

When we tune in to our own responses and express our own responses and follow our own responses, we will guide ourselves. When we feel our own responses, we are able to follow them and be guided by them to what is right for us, what is most in harmony with who and how we really are.

Feeling our own responses, expressing our own responses and following them allows us to live our own lives fully and freely. Feeling and centering our attention in our own responses gives us the power to live our lives fully and freely and this changes our whole way of being and relating to our world. When we feel our own responses and follow them, we are in control of our self and our own life. When we feel our own responses, we are in sync with our self and can guide ourselves effectively through life.

Control is the reason for all forms of oppression. We even do it in our most intimate relationships under the guise of commitment. "If you really love me, you will be who I want you to be and do what I want you to do".

Hiding our bodies and suppressing our natural responses is about control and not holiness. We live in a society that teaches us to hide and suppress our bodies and our real responses so that we will control ourselves and fit ourselves into the false and limiting beliefs of our society. This is social control being marketed as holy. This is the wolf in sheep's clothing.

The belief that we must suppress our sexual responses to be good is about control and not about being good. We say we believe in our right to be free and to express our self freely while we participate in the imposition of false beliefs on one another. We impose beliefs on one another and prevent ourselves from being who and how we really are and from living freely and fully.

Our Constitution guarantees our right to be how we are, to express ourselves freely and to live freely and yet we continue to deny this right to ourselves and one another by imposing these false and limiting beliefs on one another. We reject and punish one another for being the way we really are, for expressing our thoughts and feelings freely and for relating freely to one another, especially sexually. We suppress our self and oppress others and perpetuate a society that believes in and practices the oppression and suppression of who we really are. We are how we are by birth and by the design of the Universe and when we suppress our self, we block ourselves from being how we really are and how we were created to be. We can only be how we are and express our self freely if we accept ourselves and stop imposing our socially fabricated beliefs on one another.

Controlling our self and others in allegiance to the socially fabricated beliefs is a rejection of our right to be how we really are. If we impose our beliefs on one another, our life and our relationships are based in tyranny, control and domination and this creates relationships based in ownership, possession and domination. This can never create relationships that are open, honest, free, intimate or fulfilling.

If you get some sense of satisfaction when you suppress yourself, you are use to controlling your self. If you enjoy imposing your beliefs on others, you are controlling them. We can act politely and appropriately, according to the prevailing social beliefs but if we are not feeling or expressing our who we really are, our real responses openly, honestly and freely, we are not free. If we are suppressing our self or oppressing others, we are denying our right to be who we really are in exchange for a socially fabricated belief in tyranny and oppression. We may gain the world but we lose our self. As Werner Erhard said, "A transformed person is a person who can tell the truth and a transformed society is one in which the truth can be told."

CHAPTER 29

Right/Wrong Paradigm

———— ∞ ————

WE ARE ALL LOST IN the illusion of "right and wrong" because we have been taught to believe in the socially fabricated belief in right and wrong and it is woven into our thinking and dictates the way we relate to one another. We are living in a socially fabricated movie of right and wrong, judging life and dividing reality into right and wrong categories. We think some parts of us are good and other parts of us are bad, so we accept some things and reject other things. In this right/wrong view of reality, life is divided into what is good and bad about everyone. We believe being sexual is bad and being celibate is good. We think our beliefs are good and other people's beliefs are bad. We think others are wrong for being the way they are and we are better for being the way we are. We think we are right and that it is our duty to convince others that we are right and they are wrong. We think we are right and that we have the right to force others to agree with us or at least, do what we want them to. We think we are right, so we think we are justified in using whatever force is necessary to force others to follow what we believe and we think we have a right to demand obedience to what we think is right.

In the illusion of right and wrong, we learn our role in the social script of right and wrong, what words are right and what words are wrong, what behaviors are right and what behaviors are wrong. We are allowed to talk about some things but not others. Sexual words like fuck, cock, pussy, clitoris are seen as dirty, offensive and sinful and we are not supposed to ever say any of these words. We think it's sinful to be turned on sexually and that we are not allowed to show, say or express our sexual responses openly. In the social movie of right and wrong we think there is something wrong with us if we feel sad, hurt, or angry. In the paradigm of right and wrong, we think there is some particular way we are supposed to be that is different from how we really are. In this right/wrong belief system we reject others and blame them for our rejection because they are not being the way we think they should be. In the illusion of right and wrong we believe we have to hide our vagina, our penis, our nipples, and our anus to be good. In this illusion of right and wrong we make one another wrong and withhold our love, affection and acceptance, unless the other person bows to our demand and acts the way we want them to. In the illusion of right and wrong, our acceptance is based on whether others are being the way we want them to be and doing what we want them to do. In the illusion of right and wrong, we only love someone if they think, be and act the way we think they should think, be and act.

We learn a socially fabricated image that replaces who we really are and the authentic expression of who we really are. We cover up our real responses and do everything we can think of to make ourselves feel better. We go to meetings, take drugs, drink coffee, work out, read books, listen to tapes, eat, have sex and pray, just to feel good, but nothing really works because we are hiding and suppressing our real self.

Thinking there is something wrong with us and suppressing our self is causing the conflict we are feeling and none of our attempts to be good or right or acceptable can resolve the conflict we feel because the disturbance is being caused by our belief that there is something wrong with us.

We have become all show and no reality. Even in our closest relationships we hide our real self because we think there is something wrong with the way we are. We have become actors in our own lives, playing out some social role that we have learned, in order to be good, right and acceptable.

We are all in the same dilemma because we have all been trained to think there is something wrong with us and to hide and suppress our real self in order to fit in to these socially fabricated illusions. We are living in a society of human beings who believe there is something wrong with them, who believe in right and wrong, who believe we must hide and suppress our real responses to be good, right and acceptable and who are pretending to be like everyone else is pretending to be.

We live in a society that believes that it's beliefs about how we should be are good and how we really are is bad and we are afraid to be rejected so we reject our self to get acceptance from others.

We gain the world and lose our self or we accept our self and let go of the illusions of our society? We choose our self or the conceptual illusions of our group. It takes courage to let go of our beliefs, our illusions and our pretenses and simply be who and how we really are and give expression to all of that. It takes courage to grow up and be who and how we really are in a world of illusion.

CHAPTER 30

Non Acceptance and Pain

———— ∞ ————

WHEN WE ARE REJECTED BY our parents for not being the way they wanted us to be, we felt hurt, pain, sadness, frustration and anger, in response. When we don't accept our self or are not accepted as we really are we develop a pattern of pain and unhappiness in response to anything that seems like rejection. Our patterns of thought and reaction are dominated by our memories of being rejected and we feel all the feelings we felt then, in the present moment. We develop a pattern of pain, what Echart Tolle called the "pain body". When we are rejected by someone in the present we react with all the pain, hurt, anger and sadness of being rejected when we were young. Our thoughts can stimulate the hurt and pain and when we are rejected we think there is something wrong with some part of us, with our body, our feelings, our thinking, our sensations or our sexuality.

Who we really are is rejected by our society because our society doesn't accept our humanness and we learn to reject our self and wonder why we are unhappy and why we can't get along with others, why we don't feel okay and why we don't have easy, positive, loving relationships with others.

We feel conflict because we think there is something wrong with us and we carry this sense of "something wrong with us" into all of our relationships and our relationships are a reflection of the idea that there is something wrong with us.

Our relationships begin with positive feelings of attraction, excitement and pleasure and this energy brings us together in mutual acceptance and enjoyment but soon our patterns of thinking there is something wrong with us, that we are flawed stimulates negative feelings and reactions in our relationships because the conflict we feel in our self, stimulates this same energy in our relationships.

Our thoughts and feelings play like a movie in our mind about what is wrong with us and what we have to do to be okay. Our mind tries to guide us to being good, according to our ideas about "how we think we should be" but we are driven by our patterns of thinking there is something wrong with us. Our patterns of thinking there is something wrong with us take over and we bring all of that into our interactions with one another.

As children we thought we were being rejected because there was something wrong with us with our body, our mind, our feelings, our sexuality, so we suppressed and hid and pretended something else so we would be accepted. In the process of suppressing, hiding and pretending, we are playing out the same old patterns.

When hide and suppress ourselves and pretend to be some way we are not, we feel anxious and uncomfortable and think someone else is causing our experience because we aren't conscious of the unconscious thoughts that are causing our experience. We get stuck in our patterns of self rejection and wanting acceptance from others because we are not accepting our self. We focus on the acceptance of others, the way we did with our parents and think that someone else is the source of us feeling good or feeling bad.

Our pattern of self rejection and looking for acceptance from others plays out in all of our relationships. We look to someone else for our sense of well being and happiness, just as we looked to our parents for acceptance, love and approval. This keeps us in a struggle with our self, not feeling okay with our self and looking to others to accept us, rather than fulfilling our self by being who we really are and doing what feels right to us.

Our social conditioning teaches us to believe that there is something wrong with us and changing this belief is one of the most important things we can do to free ourselves to be who and how we really are.

This is a simple but not easy because we have to accept our self as we really are and change our patterns of hiding, suppressing and pretending and see that we are perfect manifestations of the Universe in human form.

Our learned patterns of hiding, suppressing and pretending are causing our conflict, stress, pain, suffering and is why we are in conflict with our self and one another. Our patterns of thinking there is something wrong with us are just patterns of thought that we learned in growing up in a society that is lost in these socially fabricated beliefs. There is nothing wrong with us and there never was. We are perfect manifestations of the Universe, exactly the way we are. We are human beings, living in a world of illusion.

CHAPTER 31

Criticism and Judgment

— ⌘ —

CRITICISM, BLAME AND JUDGMENT IS part of the social indoctrination we receive in learning to reject our self and others. Blame and judgment is a way of rejecting some part of our self, some part of others or some part of reality that we think should be different than it is. Whether we are criticizing our self or others, we are rejecting reality, as it is. We express our rejection of reality through blame, criticism and judgement. We argue and kill one another over our different beliefs about reality, while reality continues being what it is, regardless of our beliefs and opinions. We try to get reality to conform to our beliefs but it doesn't. As Byron Katie has said, "If you argue with reality you lose 100% of the time".

Our beliefs are like movies in our mind, playing continuously which we confuse with the reality of who we really are and our actual ongoing experience. We believe the movie playing in our mind is real and it obscures the experience we are actually having. We pretend and play a role in the socially fabricated movie and think we are being real and we are so familiar with playing our part in the social movie we feel more comfortable with "the illusion of how we should be" than "how we really are".

When we accept our self, our responses, our physical body, our emotions, our sensations and our unique way of being, we begin to experience our own reality, as it is happening in us. We are the energy of the Universe in human form and we are each having our own unique experience of it. We can accept our actual experience or we can continue to live in the socially fabricated movie of "how we should be" and this is really our only choice. We can focus on the movie in our mind or we can focus on our actual responses.

Sigmund Freud said, "Since the beginning of civilization mankind has had but one choice; to conform or not to conform. Should he choose to conform his life is over for every decisions he makes from cradle to grave will be determined by society-at-large. If he chooses not to conform, he buys himself one more choice; to be become outlaw or hero." This really is our only choice, to be who we really are or to pretend to be someone we are not to fit into the socially fabricated movie.

We live in a society that thinks beliefs are real and teaches us to reject our real self, our real way of being, our bodies, our sexuality, our feelings and our thoughts. We fear our own responses because they may reveal some part of us that is seen as bad by our society. Expressing our self openly and freely is seen as bad, wrong, sinful and unacceptable so expressing our real responses brings up our fear of being rejected. We are taught to reject our real self and to pretend behaviors that fit into the socially fabricated beliefs about how we should be. In this world of illusion expressing ourselves openly, honestly and freely is seen as radical, eccentric, unholy, unhealthy and unnatural.

CHAPTER 32

Imposing Our View

—⁕—

IMPOSITION OF ANY KIND IS a violation, a form of tyranny, oppression. When we impose our beliefs on anyone we are violating them and imposing our limited view of reality onto who they really are. We are lost in the illusion that we know better than the Universe how everyone should be. Imposing our ideas on one another is the only real offense we commit against one another and we are offending the right we each have to be who we really are and have our own experience and view.

We are each an integral part of the Universe, manifesting as we have been designed to manifest and we can't change that but we can accept it. When we impose our beliefs on one another we are not accepting reality the way it is.

We are each having our own responses and they are guiding each of us in our own experience of life. We are each a unique aspect of the Universe, manifesting the way it is designed to manifest in human form. There is no one way that is the way or truth for everyone. We are all unique in form and way of being and we are all an equal and integral part of the Universe.

Expressing ourselves openly, honestly and freely is seen as radical, eccentric, unholy, unhealthy and unnatural because we have lived in these fabricated social illusions about right and wrong for so long. Polygamy is not better than monogamy. Dark is not better than light. Blue is not better than red. Christian is not better than Muslim. Young is not better than old. Female is not better than male. Nothing is better than anything else. Everything is an equal and integral part of the Universe happening the way it is supposed to happen. There is nothing wrong with anyone or anything. Everyone is perfect, and unique, exactly the way we all are.

The Universe is made up of an infinite variety of forms and we are all unique in our way of being and functioning and we are all having our own unique responses and experience of life. What turns us on is unique to each of us. We are different in skin color, language, pronunciation, emotional intensity, tonal quality, body shape, hair texture and neurobiological functioning. We are all unique, depending on genetics, environment and social influences in which we have been reared. We like different things, eat different things, ingest different substances, have different inclinations, different desires and different interests. We have different feelings, sensations, images and responses and they are all integral parts of the Universe, as it is, in all its varied forms.

We are not meant to be the same, look the same, act the same, see the same or have the same responses. We are all meant to be uniquely the way we are, in form, energy, and function and no belief or illusion will change that. Imposing our beliefs on one another is tyranny and is causing the conflicts we experience in our self and with one another.

All systems of thought, all views, all beliefs, all philosophies, are merely concepts about reality and not the reality of how we really are. Trying to impose some system of thought onto the infinite variations of reality is a travesty of cosmic proportions. We are all part of the Universe happening and the energy of the Universe can't be contained or controlled by a conceptual belief system, no matter how wonderful we think it is.

There is no holy book, no scripture, no belief system, no philosophy, no religion, no psychology, no model, that can ever define or control the reality of how we are because we are all unique forms of the Universe manifesting in form and we are exactly the way we are meant to be by the design of the Universe.

When we center our attention in our self, in what is happening in us, in our own responses, our own energy, our own feelings, our own sensations, our own perceptions, we are centered in the Universe, as it is happening in us. When we are totally centered in our own experience, we feel the energy of the Universe that is moving through us in the movement of every molecule of our being and it is perfect and we are perfect, exactly the way we are. We are the energy of the Universe happening in physical form, along with everyone and everything else and when we tune into the energy that is happening in us and all around us, we are experiencing reality directly.

CHAPTER 33

Common Beliefs

———⟨≈≈⟩———

EVERY CULTURE HAS BELIEFS THAT have been handed down from generation to generation, the most common of which is that there is something wrong with us that we must change or fix or hide or suppress. This socially fabricated belief is a complete rejection of how we are and how we were created to be by this energy we call the Universe. From this belief comes many beliefs that we are flawed, our sexuality is bad, our emotions are bad, we must hide our bodies and that we must suppress all of our natural responses especially our sexual responses.

We are taught to believe we are separate from the energy of the Universe, which is impossible and illogical. We are part of the Universe and we can't get out of that no matter what we think or do. We human beings make up stories about God and the Universe and then make up the story that our stories come from God, a story that we made up. We think we are separate from this energy we call God so we feel separate and are afraid and don't realize we are this energy, that we are God in human form.

God is a word we use to refer to the energy of the Universe. We try to understand and explain the energy of the Universe so we can feel secure, survive and prosper. We make up these stories and have lost site of the fact that we are the ones making up the stories. We have created different words, in different languages to refer to the energy of the Universe like God, Allah, Krishna, Shiva, Elokim, Abraxas, Great Spirit, Jehovah, Yahweh, Buddha, Om, Wave and many others but this energy is what it is regardless of our name for it and we are a manifestation of this energy regardless of our beliefs or opinions about it. Regardless of what we call it or how we explain it, this energy is manifesting as us, exactly the way it is and it doesn't fit into our beliefs about it.

We are all an integral part of the Universe and we aren't separate from the Universe. We are the physical manifestation of the energy of the Universe and we are one of the many forms of the Universe, as it is manifesting in physical form. We are a part of the Universe, in fact, we are the Universe, just like the cells of our body, are our body.

We have been taught to believe that we are separate from this energy, that we are the cell but not the body, that the whole is good but the cell is not. We are taught to believe that this energy is perfect but we are not and that we are not perfect manifestations of this Universal energy.

Human beings made up the story that we are flawed and that some parts of us is not okay, even though we were created by this energy, with all of our body parts, feelings and sensations of pleasure and pain. We believe that the way we are is the imperfect manifestation of this perfect being. We believe our bodies and our sexuality are not perfect manifestation of this being we call God. We do not accept that we are the perfect manifestation of this energy or that we are this energy, in human form.

Our beliefs are in the way of us accepting ourselves as we are and that we are this energy, in human form.

Our belief that there is something wrong with us prevents us from accepting and loving our self and one another as we are. We believe we are flawed so we can't accept ourselves as we are. We believe everyone must fit into our socially fabricated beliefs to be acceptable and worthy of love and acceptance, so we judge one another and reject one another. This is one of those illogical ideas based in the illusion that there is something wrong with us and that we must hide and suppress ourselves to be okay.

This belief defies logic and yet, most of us are deeply convinced that our beliefs about how we "should be" are real, good and honorable and we actually think our beliefs are better than the reality of how we are created to be. This is a monumental illusion created by human beings and is really, "The Greatest Illusion Ever Told".

We reject who and how we really are in homage to these beliefs and lose ourselves in the process. We give up who we really are and how we really are and follow these socially fabricated beliefs in exchange for acceptance and approval by others. We reject our self and one another because we think there is something wrong with us and this prevents us from being real with one another and creating truly open, honest and intimate relationships with one another.

Our beliefs are in the way of us accepting how we really are and we have lost our connection to how we really are and we are out of touch with our real responses and have gotten lost in the rituals we perform to be good and holy. In stead of seeing we are already the perfect manifestations of the energy of the

Universe we hide and suppress ourselves to fit into these false and limiting beliefs.

We are perfect manifestations of the energy of the Universe and we have to accept this if we are to free ourselves from the bondage of these false beliefs. In the gospel of Thomas Jesus was quoted as saying, "if you will know yourself you will be known and you will see that it is you who are the manifestation of the living spirit and if you will not know this you dwell in poverty for it is you who are this poverty." We are the manifestation of the energy of the Universe that some call God and it is up to us to realize this truth.

Our physical body, our feelings, our sensations and our thoughts are all aspects of how we are created to be in our human form. Our responses are us happening and when we express our real responses, openly and honestly we open to who we really are and our relationships unfold naturally from the truth of our real beings and our interactions flow easily and naturally from the expression of who we really are.

We layer belief on top of belief, illusion on top of illusion about how we should be and all of our thoughts and behaviors come from the socially fabricated belief that there is something wrong with us. All of our fears are deeply engrained in our conditioned way of thinking so we follow the prevailing beliefs of our culture to feel safe and secure. We fear letting go of these socially fabricated beliefs and tuning in to our self and following our own inner responses, instincts, awareness and knowing.

I didn't know beliefs were just illusions. I was indoctrinated into these beliefs and I didn't trust my self or know that I am perfect, just the way I am. I was afraid of being rejected. "Will I be okay? Will anyone love me or accept me? Will I be able to get along with others, make money and take care of myself?" All of these thoughts and feelings have gone through me, along with feelings of not being okay and not fitting in. Now I know that we are all perfect and that I am okay and that everything I am is the perfection of the Universe in human form.

Life gets more interesting when we decide to accept our self as we are and be who we really are and follow our own inner guidance through life. All of the great teachers, Buddha, Jesus, Wicca, Lilith, Gandhi, Martin Luther King, Joan of Arc, John Lennon, Ramana Maharshi, Krishnamurti, Theraux, Emerson, Erhard and many others accepted themselves, spoke their truth and were often rejected by the society of people, in which they lived.

When we leave the belief systems of our society, we leave the society of people who still live in and according to these socially fabricated beliefs and we do sometimes get rejected but when we accept how we really are and the truth that we are perfect the way we are, it is easier to let go of the illusions and the false beliefs. Then we are free to be how we really are, express our-selves fully and freely and live our lives free of the illusions of our society.

When we are centered in our self, in our own energy, tuning into our own experience and allowing it to guide us, we are no longer bound by the beliefs and illusions of our society. The be-liefs of our society are just illusions, false beliefs pretending to be real. When we realize this, we are no longer bound to these illusions or lost in them. Then we are free to be who we already are, human beings who are living in a world of illusion.

Buddha has been quoted as saying, "Be a light unto yourself, be your own candle".

We are the manifestation of this energy and when we are centered in our self, tuned into the energy within us, the energy of the Universe that we are, we feel it, sense it and know it. We are the energy of the Universe and we are perfect in every way. When we center in our self, experiencing the energy that we are, we feel our connection to the energy of the Universe, which is in us and all around us.

Once we see that our beliefs about how we are supposed to be are just conceptual illusions, false ideas pretending to be real, it is easier to let them go. It's like learning how a magician does his trick. When we know what is really going on, we see through the illusion and we realize there is nothing wrong with us and we stop feeling guilty and ashamed and accept how we really are and enjoy the experience of being who we really are. Once we realize that all the stories and beliefs of our society are just conceptual illusions about life, we can let them go and embrace our self and one another, just as we are.

Accepting our self is the only thing that really changes our experience of reality. The act of accepting our self just the way we are, shifts our perception, our energy and our relationship with everyone. When we let go of our belief that there is something wrong with us we begin to relax into the experience we are having and we begin to feel harmony in our self and with our self and in our relating with others.

We are all the chosen ones by the simple fact of our existence. We are all perfect manifestations of the energy of the universe, exactly the way we are. There is nothing wrong with us and we don't need to change anything about us to be good or better. There is no better. We are already perfect the way we are. There is only the reality of how we already are, in all the different ways that we are manifesting. You are the way you are and you can't change that, even if you want to and certainly not because you believe there is something wrong with you. When we accept our self in all our differing ways of being, we can relax and enjoy our self and one another, exactly as we are.

CHAPTER 34

Beliefs, Expectations and Relationships

—— ∞∞∞ ——

BECAUSE WE GROW UP BEING indoctrinated into socially fabricated beliefs and ways of acting that are patterned from the society around us, we develop ideas and expectations that others should fit into these same social beliefs. Since we all have slightly different scripts our expectations are different and living together in close relationships, we create upsets and conflicts because we don't fit into one another's scripted beliefs.

If I expect you to be some way, other than the way you are, you will feel it as criticism, judgment, non acceptance and pressure to fit into my expectations of you. If I expect you to fulfill my expectations you will react to my expectations with resistance. If you expect me to be some way other than the way I am, I will react with resistance. This is a natural response to someone pushing us or trying to impose on us but we also react with fear to this pressure and hide and suppress ourselves in fear of rejection.

We are all having our own experience, regardless of our expectations of one another and our expectations are in the way of us being who and how we really are with one another. We suppress, hide and deny our real responses because we are trying to fit into one another's expectations and because we can't, we feel annoyed and resentful toward one another. The consequent irritation we feel causes us to hide ourselves and pull away, psychologically, emotionally, and physically. We feel hurt, offended and angry because of the pressure to hide or suppress or pretend to be different that we are.

When we let go of our expectations and accept our self and others the way we really are, we create a safe atmosphere in which we can be how we really are and enjoy one another. When we accept our real responses and allow them to guide our interactions, our relationships flow from the open, honest and spontaneous expression of our real responses. When we are just present with one another, accepting our self and one another, the pressure and resentments simply disappear and there is a sense of freedom and permission to express our real responses and share them openly and honestly. When we drop our expectations, our interactions are stimulated by our spontaneous responses to one another in the moment. All this comes from the simple act of letting go of our beliefs and expectations and accepting our self and one another, as we really are.

There is no control or domination in this way of being and relating. When we act according to some conceptual belief, we restrict ourselves and one another. In trying to impose our beliefs on one another, we cause problems and create relationships of conflict. Our expectations and demands do not support us in feeling safe to be how we really are or to express ourselves openly, honestly, fully and freely. Our false beliefs and consequent expectations limit us in what we are willing to express or show or how we are allowed to be with one another. This is mutual bondage and slavery to a set of beliefs that aren't real and are interfering in our relationships.

We have been taught to think that if we are really committed to one another we have to alter ourselves and play out some social ritual. We are taught to believe that if we play out these ways of acting we will create relationships of certainty and security. This way of relating creates conflict in us and in our relationships because it is based in imposition of our beliefs, mutual expectation and demands for us to be different than we really are. This is devastating to us and our relationships because it is so repressive, limiting, painful and unfulfilling and although we don't like it, we continue relating this way because we were trained to think this is the way to have a stable relationship and in doing so, we make our self and one another miserable.

When we accept our self and others, the way we really are, we are free to be who and how we really are and really enjoy one another, feeling and expressing ourselves openly, honestly, fully and freely.

What a revelation, what an incredible lightness of being, to just be how we really are and relate with one another, openly, honestly and freely. When we accept how we really are, we enjoy our self, alone or together, with our real responses and our authentic expression of them. This is only possible when we accept our self and others, the way we really are. Acceptance is the only action we can take or need to take to create a safe atmosphere in which we can create a sense of well being in our self and in our relationships with one another.

CHAPTER 35

Our Experience of Reality

———— ⌘ ————

OUR BELIEFS ABOUT REALITY STIMULATE our responses to what we are thinking, in the same way watching a movie at the theater stimulates our responses. The movie we are watching in our mind is stimulating our feelings, sensations and thoughts in the same way watching a movie does. When we watch the movie in our mind, over and over, we stimulate patterns of thought, feelings, sensations and behaviors. Our patterns of thought are stimulating our pattern of energetic responses and this creates our patterns of interacting with one another. We are watching the movie in our own mind and it is stimulating our sensations and feelings and consequently the experiences we are having.

The movie we are watching in our mind stimulates the energy we are feeling and this energy is felt by others, who respond to our energy and their own movie is triggered with all the consequent reactions. If our movie is critical and judgmental, it creates a pattern of negativity in our relationships. If our movie is accepting and loving it stimulates a pattern of positive energy in our relationships.

When we are living and responding from the movie in our mind, the experiences we are creating reinforce our patterns of thought, belief and experience and thus our perception of reality. When people believed the world was flat, they couldn't see that it was round. Believing is seeing in this case. What we believe creates what we see.

When we believe that there is something wrong with us, we create the consequent conflict and disturbances we feel. Our beliefs are ideas we think over and over again, creating our mind's movie, which stimulates our responses and consequently, our interactions with others and reinforcing what we think. When we believe we or someone else is wrong, we judge our self or one another as bad and thus we create conflict and struggle in our self and in our relationships.

The belief that there is something wrong with us is the movie into which we were born and indoctrinated and our patterns of conflict created by this belief continue, even when we feel love for one another. We try to change our self and one another to what we have been taught to believe we should be and this belief in right and wrong plays out in all of our relationships and is creating the conflict and disturbance we are experiencing.

Our learned judgements about our bodies, our sexuality and our emotions are stimulating all of our conflict and as long as we do not accept how we really are, we will continue to stimulate conflict in our self and in our relationships with one another. The problems we are having, we are creating because of our belief in the socially indoctrinated movie that there is something wrong with us and we have to let go of this belief to resolve our conflicts. We are not meant to suppress our self or oppress one another but this is what we are trained to do by our society.

We are designed to by nature to be fully alive, to tune into our own responses, let them guide us and express ourselves freely, like the sun, the wind, the water, the plants, the insects, the animals or the stars. We are here to feel, sense and perceive our own experience of reality and to interact with one another according to our actual responses.

We have been oppressing one another, dominating one another, controlling one another and harming one another for most of human history and it is apparent that oppression and suppression doesn't stimulate happy, alive, vital, joyful experiences for us but because of our socially fabricated beliefs we continue to create conflict in our self and with one another.

To change this we have to let go of our belief that there is something wrong with us and get out of the movie in our mind, stop suppressing our responses and stop imposing our beliefs and expectations on one another.

Becoming aware of the movie in our mind and seeing it for the illusion that it is and allowing our real responses to be felt and expressed frees us to feel and express what we are really experiencing and to create relationships of mutual acceptance, love, respect and real intimacy.

Accepting our self and others is a choice that we can make once we are aware of the social movie that has been running us. Accepting our self and others is a conscious decision that we must make to change our own perception, our own energy and the way we relate to one another.

We have a choice of living in the socially fabricated movie or accepting ourselves the way we really are. By accepting our self as we really are, we stop living in the movie about how we should be and we stop imposing these false beliefs and expectations on our self and on one another. We must choose to accept our self and let go of the socially fabricated illusion and we must shift our attention to who and how we really are, to our real responses, if we are to escape the social illusions and the conflict they are creating.

When we stop imposing our beliefs and expectations on one another, we start living authentically and fully but we must let go of the socially fabricated movie in our mind that we have been watching our whole life and accept our real responses and begin to relate openly, honestly, and freely, without imposition, pressure or conflict if we are to live freely, easily and enjoyably.

Life is perfect as it is and we are perfect as we are. The real issue we face, is whether we accept our self or reject our self, as we are, whether we let go of the movie in our mind and accept reality, as it is, whether we continue living in oppression and suppression or accept ourselves as we really are.

There is nothing holy or healthy about oppression and suppression of our true nature. Suppressing our self and oppressing others is against life, against nature and against the Universe, of which we are but one form.

CHAPTER 36

Beliefs & Illusion

———— ⤫ ————

WE ARE LIVING IN A social movie about reality that isn't real, that is simply a socially fabricated illusion and we reinforce this illusion by participating in it. As long as we believe these false beliefs and live our lives according to them, as if they are real, we perpetuate in these illusions, as if they are real. Our ideas about reality are not the same as reality. Living in the social belief that some part of us is bad or wrong, is living in the idea that the Universe is wrong for being the way it is.

We are the reality of the Universe happening, in human form, just the way we are. We either accept our self the way we are or we live in the socially fabricated beliefs that say we are wrong for being the way we are. We accept our self or not. Accepting ourselves as we really are brings us into harmony with our self and one another and non acceptance creates conflict. We are living in the socially fabricated beliefs or we are living in our own direct experience.

We have lived according to these beliefs for so long we have difficulty seeing them for the illusions they are. We have been lost as individuals and as a society, in these socially fabricated illusions for so long, we have a hard time extricating ourselves from them and seeing they are just illusions. We have to see that the movie in our mind isn't reality. Just as we once believed the earth was flat we must let go of our belief that there is something wrong with us if we are to become fully aware of the truth of who we are and become fully functional human beings, if we are to create a society that is real and truly healthy and happy.

Reality is simply the way something is. Reality is how we really are. Accepting our self as we really are, is the only way out of the beliefs, out of the illusions, out of the social movie and out of the conflict we are experiencing in our self and with one another.

Ralph Waldo Emerson said, "It takes a great deal of courage to grow up and be who we really are". It takes courage to be how we really are and express our self authentically in a world that is still living in the socially fabricated belief that there is something wrong with us. It takes courage to be how we really are in a world that doesn't accept how we really are. It takes courage to be who we really are and express our real responses, as they are, openly, honestly, fully and freely in this world of illusion.

Staying within these socially fabricated beliefs may get us acceptance by others but we lose our real self and give up who and how we really are. This is why so many of us don't know what we are feeling, thinking or what we really want. We don't know when something feels good or doesn't. We learn to override our own responses to fit into the social beliefs, rather than feeling what we are actually feeling and giving expression to our real responses. The price for staying in the socially fabricated illusion, is the loss of our real self and losing touch with our real responses and losing our ability to express ourselves fully or freely.

The reward for leaving the socially fabricated illusion, is being real, being who and how we really are and expressing ourselves openly, honestly, and fully in a state of harmony, clarity, ease and enjoyment. We can tune into our real responses or we can continue to play the socially created role we have learned to play. Like Neo, in the movie, The Matrix, we each have a choice between two different worlds and we must choose for our self, which one we live in. Each of us is making our own choice. The illusion of socially fabricated beliefs or the reality of our own experience of reality, our real way of being.

CHAPTER 37

The Role of Social Institutions

———⋙⋘———

SOCIAL INSTITUTIONS ARE SYSTEMS OF conditioning and control that perpetuate themselves by indoctrinating us into the beliefs of our society. Governments, religions, schools, police, military, corporations, clubs, associations, corporations, all indoctrinate us into the prevailing social beliefs, teaching us to suppress our own individual responses and to limit our expression of our real self and limit our expression to what fits into the socially fabricated illusions.

The view that there is some part of us that is not okay, that must be denied, hidden and suppressed is a denial of who we really are and yet is taught by most social institutions. We are a perfect part of the Universe exactly the way we are, regardless of the beliefs perpetuated by these institutions but the institutions maintain control of their members by establishing and perpetuating a particular belief system.

The creative force of the Universe is already manifesting in all of these different ways, including you and me and everyone and everything and none of it fits into our beliefs perpetuated by our institutions about how we should be. We are creation happening, just the way we are our beliefs about it are just ideas that do not represent reality.

The beliefs perpetuated by our social institutions are beliefs passed on from previous generations that have become part of the social movie playing in our minds that dominates the thinking of the leaders of social institutions who are simply passing on what they have been indoctrinated into and perpetuate through the teachings that they have learned.

Jesus, Socrates, Lao Tsu, Buddha, Mohamed, Krishnamurti and many others, saw through the illusions of their cultural teachings and saw that we are all perfect manifestations of the universe in human form and they did their best to communicate this simple truth but this didn't fit into the beliefs of their social institutions and they were shunned by the people of their time.

The realization that we are perfect manifestations of the energy of the Universe frees us from these false and limiting beliefs of our culture. Jesus said,"God is within us". Buddha said, "be your own candle, be a light unto your self." Lao Tsu taught that, "The Way" is already happening and that we are part of that happening and that we simply have to let go into it. Socrates taught his students to follow their own inner guidance and to ignore the beliefs of their culture.

When we are being real, being who we really are and expressing ourselves openly, honestly and authentically, we are in harmony with ourselves and we feel good inside because we are being real and expressing our real self. When we express what we are really feeling, thinking, sensing, we are integrated, centered, and fully alive because we are being real and living our lives fully and freely as we really are.

No one who is being true to who they really are, true to their own experience of reality can live according to any socially fabricated beliefs. The teachers of truth did not live their lives according to the beliefs of their social institutions because they saw that these beliefs were the illusions of their society. These individuals were having their own direct experience of reality and tried to awaken everyone to the truth of who we really are, to our own experience, our own divinity, our own perfect manifestation of this energy that is within us, that some call God. They taught the simple truth that God is within us and that we are the energy of the Universe manifesting in human form.

Religious teachings have been especially confusing for most of us because we have been taught to believe these social institutions and the beliefs they teach are the truth and it's difficult for most of us to see that they are not true, that in fact they are the illusions of the social institutions that have been passed on from generation to generation, what have been referred to as "sins of the fathers".

Beliefs are the accumulated ideas of society and the institutions of our society, mental pictures about reality taught as the truth, that are limited perceptions of reality that restrict us in how we see ourselves and how we allow ourselves to be.

Religions have been our primary social institutions created to indoctrinate everyone into the prevailing beliefs of society. The primary teaching is that some part of us is flawed, sinful and unacceptable to God and must be hidden and suppressed for us to be acceptable to God. We are mesmerized by these beliefs even though they just someone's idea about how we should be. These beliefs are the illusions created in the minds of human beings a long time ago and perpetuated by social institutions as if they are the truth and they separate us from who we really are and from our own personal experience of existence.

Leaders of social institutions indoctrinate us into these beliefs because they were also indoctrinated into these beliefs. Social institutions use stories and rituals to indoctrinate us into these beliefs and reward and punishment to condition us into behaving according to these beliefs. We are indoctrinated and conditioned with threats, ridicule, intimidation and abused if we do not adhere to the beliefs being taught and we are ostracized, shunned and excommunicated if we do not adhere to the teachings.

While we are taught to believe we are all 'endowed by our creator" with certain unalienable rights to live freely, leaders of social institutions use whatever force they can to force everyone into compliance with these socially fabricated beliefs. In the past, leaders of social institutions had enormous power and dominated with violence and aggression. They simply killed anyone who did not go along with their beliefs. Now leaders of social institutions use intimidation, threats, ridicule and rejection to pressure everyone into following the prevailing social beliefs.

Expressing what we are really feeling and thinking, our real responses, as they are moving through us is natural and we feel more alive with the energy of our own life when we are expressing what we are actually experiencing. Our energy, our real responses, our feelings and sensations are not meant to be suppressed, hidden and inhibited and yet that is what we are taught to do. When we suppress our own energy, we are blocking our energy and it builds up in intensity until we can't hold it back and we explode on others or implode into our self.

Whatever we suppress builds in intensity and becomes the obsessive focus of our attention. We become obsessed with whatever we are suppressing because it is still moving in us and it builds in intensity below the surface of our suppression. We may be hiding what we are feeling behind a smokescreen of pretense but the energy we are feeling is still moving in us and through us. We are having a continual flow of energy in the form of feelings and sensations that are moving through us, whether we are suppressing them or not and they will grow in intensity when we hold them in.

We human beings are just one of the many forms of the energy of the Universe, manifesting in physical form. All of the various forms of existence are the energy of the Universe happening in physical form. We are designed to be the way we are by the energy of the Universe, just as the Sun is designed to be how it is, just as the moon is designed to be how it is. Everything is exactly the way it is by the design of the Universe and is perfect, just as it is, including us.

We are perfect manifestations of the Universe exactly the way we are. Our beliefs are flawed and not us. Beliefs are only conceptual ideas about reality and not reality as it is. We have mistaken these socially fabricated beliefs for reality because we have all been trained to believe in them and we are all immersed in these illusions, as if they are real and we are living in them and according to them, as if they are real. We are the way we are by the design of the Universe with all our sexual, emotional, physical, and mental parts. Our body, our mind, our emotions, and our sexuality, are all integral aspects of our neurobiological system, designed to be exactly the way it is.

Suppressing our responses is not healthy or natural and is a denial of reality, a denial of our self as we really are and a denial of creation as it truly is. Beliefs are just ideas we have about reality and it is up to us to see this and let go of them and learn to accept ourselves and center in our self, as we really are.

We are life happening. Every molecule of our energy, every sensation, every thought, every image, every feeling, every part of our body is the perfect manifestation of the Universe, happening the way we were created to be.

The belief that there is something wrong with us is simply a false teaching that is causing all of our conflict, disturbance and anxiety. This disturbance is the result of believing the illusion that we are not okay and as long as we believe this false teaching, we will never be free to be how we really are.

When we are trying to be some way that is different then we are, we are creating conflict within us and consequently, conflict in our relationships with one another. When we accept how we really are, we begin to relax, feel at peace and in the process we create peace, harmony and enjoyment in our self and in our relationships.

These are two very different ways of seeing ourselves which leads to different ways of being and different ways of expressing and experiencing life. We are either in the socially fabricated illusion of our beliefs about how we should be or we are centered in our self and accepting our own energetic experience.

"To be or not to be," William Shakespeare said. We must choose to be how we really are or go along with the false conceptual beliefs of our society into which we have been born. We are not the way these social beliefs say we should be and yet we continue to perpetuate these beliefs and impose them on our self and one another.

We are each a unique version of creation, of life, of the Universe and we are not meant to be exactly the same or fit into any beliefs about how we should be. We are meant to be exactly the way we are, with all of our feelings, sensations, thoughts and images moving through us, in all of our unique and individualized ways of being.

All beliefs are conceptual ideas about reality, illusions. We are real, just as we are, with all our unique variations in form and energy but our beliefs about us are not. We are the reality of the Universe happening in human form and when we accept ourselves, just as we are and let go of all beliefs about how we should be, our conflicts will end. In letting go of these false beliefs and leaving these socially fabricated illusions we can tune into our real experience of reality and enjoy the pure experience of life itself, as it really is and as we really are.

CHAPTER 38

Leaving the Illusion

———— ⟋⟍⟋ ————

To LEAVE THE ILLUSIONS OF our socially fabricated beliefs, we must see that they are just ideas that we were taught to believe that were created by the minds of human beings. Then we must accept our self completely, as we really are and we must centered in our self, in our own responses, our own energy, our own feelings, sensations and experience. By centering in our own responses and accepting them as they are, we are directly connected to our real self and not focused in the movie in our mind and the socially fabricated beliefs of our society. When we center in our self and are aware of our own responses and accepting them as they are, we are able to leave the socially fabricated illusions and are no longer mesmerized by the movie in our mind.

This starts with the awareness that the beliefs we have inherited are only conceptual ideas and not the reality of our own natural way of being. Then we must make a conscious choice to tune into our own natural responses and to accept them and our self, as we really are, with all the responses we are having.

We must make a conscious decision to accept our own responses in order to get centered in our self and let go of the socially driven movie playing in our mind. We must see this and make this decision for our self. No one can make this decision for us. In accepting our self as we really are, we allow our self to be who and how we really are and we let go of the movie playing in our mind and the socially fabricated beliefs of our culture.

Acceptance is the key to freeing ourselves from the idea that there is something wrong with us and thus resolving all of the conflict we are experiencing in our self and in our relationships with one another. When we accept all of these different forms of energy that are moving through us, we begin to relax into our self, into the experience we are having and then we are able to allow ourselves to be how we really are and are able to express our real responses, as they are happening in us and then we can relate authentically with one another. When we are fully centered in our own being, our own awareness, our own responses, accepting them and allowing them to be whatever they are and are able to express them freely, we are out of the socially fabricated illusions of our mind and centered in the reality that is happening within us.

Our energetic responses are already happening in us and all we have to do is tune into them, accept them and allow them to be how they are. To do this we must make the decision to accept everything about our self, our whole experience, our physical body, our feelings, our sensations, our thoughts, our fantasies, our sexuality and our own individual way of being. We have to accept all of our self.

We especially have to accept our sexuality and our enjoyment of sexual pleasure because this is a part of us that has been seen as wrong and has been rejected by our society for thousands of years and we have to reclaim all aspects of our being, including our feelings and our sexuality. We are sexual beings, as is the whole world of beings around us and we have to accept our sexual energy and our desire for sexual pleasure.

Our feelings, sensations and thoughts are all aspects of our natural neurobiological system, functioning perfectly, just as it was designed to function by the energy of the Universe. We are the Universe happening in physical form. Our feelings, visions, thoughts, sensations, sexuality, images, dreams, desires, fantasies, and physical bodies are all aspects of the Universe happening, in human form. We have to accept our self exactly the way we are and accept that we are the energy of the Universe in human form and that we are each having our own individual experience of existence, with feelings, sensations and sexual parts that are all part of what it is to be a being human.

The socially fabricated belief that there is something wrong with us or any part of us is the primary illusion that we must be aware of, in order to dispel this illusion and accept ourselves as we really are. The belief that there is something wrong with our bodies, our emotions, our sexuality, our penis, our clitoris, our vagina, our nipples or our anus, is a false belief pretending to be real, which is the definition of an illusion.

We are all perfect manifestations of the Universe in human form and we must accept this if we are to release ourselves from the false ideas of our culture. When we see that our beliefs are just conceptual ideas about reality, we can begin to retrain our self to accept how we really are and begin living our lives fully and freely, centered in our own responses. When we are centered in our own responses we see the socially fabricated illusion and it begins to disappear like the mirages they are.

When we are in the socially fabricated illusion, we feel disturbed because our own experience of reality is in conflict with the illusion. We feel uncomfortable because we are not aligned with the socially fabricated illusion. Our discomfort is a reaction from our own neurobiological system telling us that something is not in sync, not in harmony with us or reality. Our discomfort is a signal from our own neurobiological guidance system letting us know something isn't true and that we are out of sync with reality. When we center in our own energy, our own responses and accept them, as they are, we begin to experience the integration of our own awareness of reality, as it is and with what is actually happening in our self.

As we become more familiar with being centered in our own personal experience of reality, we begin to feel comfortable and in harmony with our self and our world. As we learn to be centered in our own responses our socially learned patterns of suppressing our responses begins to dissipate and the illusions in our mind begin to lose their influence over our reactions and our behavior. Then we are able to be how we really are and feel our own responses as they really are and be fully human as we are meant to be.

CHAPTER 39

Our Personal Version of the Social Illusion

———— ⌘ ————

WE HAVE TO FACE OUR own personal version of the illusion in our mind if we are to release it and free ourselves to be who we really are. We each grow up in a society that has beliefs about how we have to be to be good and we each develop our own beliefs based in these social illusions. Seeing our own version of the social movie may seem difficult at first, but we can see it by watching the movie in our mind as if we are in a movie theater. With practice we can see that the movie in our mind is just a movie and that we are the one watching the movie. Then we can see the difference between the social movie playing in our mind and we are able to refocus on our own sensations and feelings, that are not being generated by the movie in our mind. We have to make a conscious effort to see the movie playing in our mind and shift our attention from the movie in our mind to our real responses. This begins with seeing the difference and making a decision to accept our real feelings and sensations as they really are.

There is a huge difference between our reactions that are being stimulated by the movie in our mind and our authentic responses that are being generated by our authentic response to what is happening in the moment. When we tune into our real responses, our actual responses stimulate our authentic responses to what is actually happening in the moment. When we do this we are able to tune in and feel our own authentic responses, rather than responding from our choreographed mental pictures and social behaviors that are the result of the illusions created by the conceptual beliefs of our society.

We are each having our own individual responses to life and when we focus our attention on our actual responses, they guide us impeccably in responding to what is happening in each moment and in each situation.

Shifting our attention out of the illusion and tuning into the reality of our own authentic responses requires a shift in our focus of attention. We are trained to focus on socially fabricate beliefs about how we should be, so noticing the difference is not easy at first because the illusions we have learned and lived in for so long seem real and dominate our thinking.

An illusion is simply a perception that appears to be real but isn't.

We are all living in our own version of these socially fabricated beliefs and we feel comfortable when we are pretending to be some way that fits into the social beliefs because it is what we are used to and is also the way everyone else is pretending to be. This mutually agreed upon belief about how we should be is being perpetuated by all of us because we have all been indoctrinated into the same beliefs about how we should be. When we live in these socially fabricated beliefs, we are playing our part in a shared social illusion about reality. When we suppress our real responses and pretend these socially fabricated responses, we are denying the reality of who we really are and this causes us to be out of sync with our real self.

When our actual responses don't fit into our conceptual beliefs, we feel conflict and we feel uncomfortable, so we tend to suppress what is really happening in us and cover it with a pretended social image.

Once we have established the socially fabricated movie in our mind, we relate and interact according to this movie that has replaced the reality of our actual responses. Our own responses continue to move in us even though we have learned to suppress them and even though we live in the socially fabricated movie in our mind but we lose touch with our actual responses and with who and how we really are. How we are pretending to be replaces who we really are and our expression of our actual responses and our interactions with one another become a socially prescribed pretension. Only when we are centered in our self do we leave the socially fabricated illusion and are able to be present with the reality of our own experience.

CHAPTER 40

Imagination

———— ⁂ ————

OUR IMAGINATION IS A NATURAL aspect of our neurobiological system showing us new possibilities and guiding us toward what we want for our own fulfillment. When we see images or visions of what we want and desire it is our own neurobiological system guiding us toward the fulfillment of our own being. Our visions, fantasies, dreams and thoughts appear in our mind, showing us possibilities of the fulfillment of our wants, desires and needs.

Our neurobiological system is designed perfectly to respond and guide us to the fulfillment of our wants, needs and desires. Our ability to see and envision what we want is an integral part of our natural biological process doing what it is designed to do in guiding us through life. Visions, images and fantasies are aspects of our own neurobiological system responding to life as it arises and guiding us to our own fulfillment. When we tune into our own sensations, feelings, thoughts, fantasies and visions, we are tuning into our own neurobiological guidance system and the guidance it is giving us. We are each having our own individual responses and we are the only one who can tune into them and know what they are showing us and guiding us to.

Ultimately, we are the energy of the universe and this energy is the experience we are having in response to life and it is guiding us to our own fulfillment. When we tune into our own energy we are guided perfectly and we realize we are not our ideas and beliefs about how we should be but the actual energy experience we are having. We can tune in to our own responses or we can tune in to our socially fabricated beliefs about how we should be. By tuning into our own energy, we connect directly to our own neurobiological systems experience of reality.

CHAPTER 41

Our Real Responses

CENTERING IN OUR OWN RESPONSES, our own energy that manifests as the sensations, feelings and images that are vibrating in us and through us is really all there is to do to experience our own experience and know what is real for us and learning to allow it to guide us through life. Being centered in our own being brings an end to our mentally constructed illusions that are causing our conflict because we are no living in or according to the illusion and no longer hiding, suppressing or pretending. Centering our attention in our own responses connects us directly with our self and with our own experience of reality. When we are centered in our own energy and following our responses, we are naturally guided in alignment with our own being.

Concepts about how we should be are not real so they are not accurate guides in our encounter with life. We can talk about our views of existence but we are each having our own experience of existence and our experience is the only experience that can give us an accurate read on what is really going on.

We are the experience we are having. We are not an idea or a belief. We are life happening and each one of us is having our own experience of life, just as we are and being centered in our own experience, we live our life fully and freely from our own responses. When we are centered in our self all conflict vanishes along with the illusions that have been creating them. Being centered in our own responses brings us into alignment with our self and therefor in harmony with our self. This is the true meaning of integrity, being one with our self, fully integrated. When we are centered in our self, our mind, our feelings, our energies are congruent and we have a sense of well being that is the result of being centered.

Centering in our own responses is an ability we develop by focusing on the energy that we are, the energy that is moving in us and through us. When we are centered in our own energy we are guided from our own inner being to what is most resonant with us.

Focusing on our inner responses, allows our inner guidance system to guide us through life, creating a stable and deeply connected experience. By centering in our own responses we leave the illusions of our conceptual mind and tune into our own personal experience of reality. In allowing our inner energy, our own responses to guide us, we end a life of conflict with our self and others.

When we center in our own experience and accept whatever that is, the conflict in us is over and we stop suffering under the illusion that there is something wrong with us or anyone else. When we accept how we are, we are free.

CHAPTER 42

The Resonance of Love

———— ✂ ————

WHEN WE ARE FREE FROM all conflict with our self and others we feel the resonance of love because love comes from the total acceptance and appreciation for life as it is. Love is a harmonic resonance of acceptance, allowance, connectedness, harmony, enjoyment, happiness, excitement, pleasure, and appreciation. Love is harmonious energy and is felt as pleasurable sensations in our body, mind and emotions. When we vibrate with the energy of love we feel pleasure in every molecule of our being and in our whole body. Our energy field lights up with this vital energy of love when we are accepting and appreciating our self and others.

Our concepts of love obscure our direct experience of the energy of love. When we are focused on our ideas about love we replace the energy of love with words, beliefs and rituals about love. We have learned to act out the rituals of love, while not actually allowing our self to feel the feelings and sensations of love. We say, "I love you" and give one another gifts as a ritual to communicate that we love one another but we do not allow ourselves to fully feel the sensations of love, vibrating in our energy and in our tissue. We express the conceptual idea of love in words rather than feeling the vibrations and sensations of love. We relate to one another in predetermined ways while not allowing our self to feel the pleasurable sensations of love.

When we are playing out social rituals of love we lose touch with our real sensations and feelings of pleasure and excitement that are the experience of love. We hide and suppress our feelings and sensations of love, while following the social rituals of words and gifts.

Social rituals do not express our feelings of love, pleasure and excitement. Our energy of love is covered up with polite rituals while we deny ourselves the direct experience of love. We live in a society that is afraid of the feelings and sensations of love and passion.

We are often ridiculed if we express love and sexual passion openly, with comments like "get a room" to embarrass us into inhibiting the open expression of love and passion. This is our societies way of rejecting love and sexuality. We ridicule one another for the open expression of our most natural response of love and wonder why we "live lives of quiet desperation" and separation and not allowing ourselves to feel the sensations and feelings of love.

When we accept and allow ourselves to actually feel the feelings and sensations of love we are filled with the energy and vitality of this natural sensation and pleasurable energy of love.

Love is a wonderful energy that feels so good when we allow ourselves to feel it and experience it deeply and fully.

CHAPTER 43

Our Mind

———— ◦◦◦ ————

OUR MIND IS THE PART of us that assesses what we are perceiving so we can make sense of life and make decisions and choices that are beneficial to our own life. Our thoughts and images appear in our mind, showing us possibilities of our own fulfillment and guiding us to experiences that fit our wants, needs and desires. This is our neurobiological system guiding us and showing us images of things and experiences of what will fulfill us. When we are hungry we see images of food. When we are turned on sexually we see images of sex. When we are tired we see images of sleeping. Our body's need for food causes sensation of hunger and our mind responds with images of what the body wants for it's fulfillment. Our mind is an integral part of our guidance system, showing us visually what we want and need to fulfill our most basic needs, wants and desires.

Our whole neurobiological system is always responding and guiding us to the fulfillment of our own wants, needs and desires, in the form of sensations, feelings and images of what might fulfill our needs, wants and desires. Our energetic responses are our neurobiological system guiding us in fulfilling ourselves.

When we suppress our mind's natural ability to see what it wants and force ourselves to focus on some socially driven concept about how we should be, we interfere with our own neuro-biological system in doing what it is designed to do.

We can tune into the images that arise in our own mind naturally and allow them to guide us if we let go of the limiting beliefs of our culture that tell us what we should want, according to the fabricated beliefs of our society.

Our mind is designed to take in, store and synthesize information to make senses of what is happening in guiding us in fulfilling our needs. Our mind observes, sees, assesses and analyzes all of it, in guiding us in making beneficial choices when it is directly connected to our own responses.

Life is happening in us, as well as around us and our mind observes and makes choices to support our own life. These images appear in our minds possible fulfillments of our life. An image of food or a place to get it appears in our mind when we are hungry, images of water when we are thirsty, someone we love when we want connection. A flying machine that has no engine and is powered by the individual flying it. A hovercraft powered by a device that absorbs energy from the field of energy in the space around it. Recycling waste back into the earth rather than putting it into our water system. Ideas appear in our mind in responses to our needs, wants and desires. "Necessity is the mother of invention."

Our mind functions perfectly when we allow it to see the images that arise in our own consciousness in response to our own real needs. Socially fabricated ideas that are not directly connected to reality, beliefs that are not connected to what is actually happening interfere with this natural process.

CHAPTER 44

Desire

——— ∞∞ ———

DESIRE IS A NATURAL PART of our neurobiological system showing us with sensations and feelings, what we want and need
physically, emotionally and sexually. The energy of desire is in
response to our neurobiological need for pleasure and fulfillment. Desire is showing us, directing us, guiding us, moving
us toward someone or something that is the fulfillment of our
needs.

Our desire for love, sex, food, water, air and other forms of
nurturance is always guiding us to the things and experiences that will fulfill us. Desire is the sensation of excitement and
pleasurable responses to someone or something that matches
our energy and is the fulfillment of our desire.

We desire food when we are hungry, water when we are
thirsty, sex when we want connection and physical pleasure with
others. Without desire we would not know what we want or need.
Desire is a natural part of our energetic response system, guiding us to what will fulfill us. We are life happening in human
form and we are designed with the energy of desire to guide us
to whatever will fulfill us.

We have been taught to believe that desire is bad or wrong and should be suppressed to maintain our image of goodness. Even in well intended spiritual teachings, desire is often seen and depicted as something to let go of, something to be suppressed and hidden in order to achieve peace, oneness or enlightenment.

We are human beings and we are designed with desire to guide us. Our sexual desire is just one aspect of this energy and when we accept our sexual desire and allow our sexual energy to be how it is, we can allow it to guide us to our own fulfillment just like we do with our desire for food when we are hungry and water when we are thirsty.

The cause of all conflict and suffering is the suppression of our natural energy, our sensations and feelings, our real self, our own natural way of being. We are designed to be the way we are, with all of our energy, with all of our sensations and the images of our own fulfillment that are moving in us and through us all the time, stimulating desire in us and moving us toward our own fulfillment.

Bruce Lipton, the great cellular biologist said that every single cell responds automatically to everything by moving toward what is beneficial to it or away from that which is not and we are a collective of single cells responding to what is beneficial to us and what is not.

We are born with eyes to see, ears to hear, noses to smell, tongues to taste, fingers to touch and genitals to feel sexual pleasure and they are all guiding us into experiences that are the fulfillment of our needs.

When we deny our own natural responses we are interfering with our neurobiological system in functioning as it is designed to function by sending us messages in the form of feelings and sensations that are guiding us to the fulfillment of our own life. When we suppress our own responses and our own desires we are interfering with our neurobiological system and preventing ourselves from functioning fully.

We are designed to be the way we are, with all of our emotions, sensations, perceptions and sexuality and we have been rejecting our self, our own body, our emotions, our sensations and our natural way of being because of a set of socially fabricated beliefs that are not based in reality.

The Universe designed us to be sexual beings, with sexual energy, sexual sensations of pleasure and sexual physical parts so we would be sexual with one another. We are created with sexual energy and sexual parts with sensations of pleasure to encourage us to come together for sexual pleasure.

We were created to be sexual, to feel sexual sensations of pleasure, to be turned on sexually to one another and to pleasure one another sexually because it connects us and stimulates us into positive relationships with one another. When we allow our sexual energy we are allowing our self to be the way we were designed to be by the Universe.

CHAPTER 45

Losing Touch With Our Responses

———— ∞ ————

WE LOSE TOUCH WITH OUR own responses because we have learned to suppress them and we lose awareness of them. When we are asked what we want many of us don't know because we have suppressed our own responses to the point that we have lost touch with this part of our guidance system. We suppress our own responses, our own neurobiological system and wonder why we are out of touch and don't know what we want or need.

We have lost touch with our own feelings and sensations and therefor our ability to tune in to this energy and allow it to guide us. We have learned to suppress our own guidance system and wonder why we don't know what it is telling us and showing us. We are asking our neurobiological system to function, while we are suppressing the responses that are the energy of our own neurobiological guidance system. We suppress, hide and inhibit our own neurobiological system from functioning and wonder why we don't know what we want and why we are so dysfunctional.

We must let go of the socially fabricated belief that there is something wrong with us and we must accept how we really are, with all of our sensations, feelings, body parts and functions, if we are to become fully functional. We have to allow ourselves to be aware of our responses and learn to follow them as they guide us in our interactions with one another. By accepting ourselves and allowing our sensations, feelings and thoughts to flow freely, we are allowing our own neurobiological system to function, as it is designed to function by the design of the energy of the Universe.

CHAPTER 46

Perfect Manifestations of Life

———— ❧ ————

WE ARE PERFECT MANIFESTATIONS OF the energy of the Universe and we are perfectly designed physically, mentally, emotionally and sexually and when we accept the way we are and allow ourselves to be the way we really are, we are able to function fully and perfectly. Our neurobiological system is perfectly designed with sensory receptors, feelings and a mind that works perfectly when we let them. Our wants, needs and desires are part of our neurobiological system guiding us to our own fulfillment and that is the way we are designed to be by this energy of the Universe that some call God.

We are taught to think that our emotions will mislead us or our sexual desire will get us in trouble and that enjoying sexual pleasure is wrong. Nothing could be further from the truth but that is the socially fabricated belief that is perpetuated in our society. We are told to hide, suppress and resist sexual desire and to pray for forgiveness for being sexual or having a sexual fantasy or for wanting sexual pleasure, as if giving our bodies the pleasures we want and are designed to feel is some unholy thing. The only unholy thing I know of is the hiding, suppressing and denial of our natural responses.

The denial of our sexual and emotional responses is the only real sin, along with the false teaching and misunderstanding of what is truly good.

CHAPTER 47

Sensations

———— ∞∞∞ ————

SENSATIONS AND FEELINGS ARE PART of our neurobiological design, guiding us toward what is beneficial or away from what is not. We are a sensory system that responds with sensations, feelings and images that guide our awareness and our actions toward what is beneficial and away from that which is harmful. Our sensations and feelings are signals from our neurobiological system, showing us what is resonant with us and what is not. When we tune into our own responses, we are tuning into our own neurobiological guidance system that is guiding us toward what is in harmony with our own being and toward the fulfillment of our needs.

Our neurobiological system is always responding and guiding us to what is most resonant with us. When we feel excited our system is telling us to go toward what is stimulating our excitement. We move toward what we like, want, desire and need and away from what is not resonant with us. We are energetic beings in a physical body with a sensory system with feelings and sensations that are always responding and guiding us in our interactions with everyone and everything in our lives.

If we accept and allow our responses to flow freely, we feel the pleasure of our own life force moving through us and learn to follow the signals it is giving us. Our responses are our life force, our vital energy, in all it's varied forms, flowing through us in response to our needs, wants and desires.

We are one of many forms of the energy of the Universe, in physical form and when we accept and allow our responses to flow freely we are guided perfectly in our interactions with our world. When we accept the responses that are moving in us, they guide us and we begin to see clearly and are able to follow our own inner guidance system to what it is showing us and we begin to enjoy our own experience of life.

Allowing our self to be how we really are and having the responses we are really having creates a feeling of aliveness, excitement and pleasure in us. Acceptance of all the different forms of our energy allows us to open ourselves and express our responses freely, fully, openly and naturally. When we accept our responses and express them fully and freely, we are able to fulfill ourselves in each moment.

CHAPTER 48

Sexual Energy

———— ∞ ————

WHEN WE ARE ATTRACTED TO one another we feel excitement and pleasurable sensations flowing through us because we are feeling the energy of life and it is vital, healthy and pleasurable. Pleasurable sensations guide us toward what is causing us to feel so good. Sensations of pleasure flow through us naturally in response to what is beneficial to us and expressing responses freely and fully is one of the most pleasurable experiences we can have.

Sex is one form of pleasure that is a natural part of our neurobiological system exciting us and bringing us together for mutual pleasure and fulfillment. When we feel the tingle of sexual energy moving through us, we open to being sexual with one another. When we allow our sexual energy to flow freely through us, we feel the vitality of our own juices flowing. Sexual energy is part of the energy of the Universe being the way it is, doing what it does, exactly the way it is supposed to.

We are the energy of the Universe manifesting in physical human form and we are designed to be sexual. Every species, every biological organism, is sexual. This is how we were designed to be and when we allow ourselves to be sexual, we are allowing the Universe to be the way it is and do what it does naturally. Being sexual is being human, being alive, being life, expressing life, expressing the natural energy of the Universe.

We are all perfect manifestation of the Universe and our sexual energy is part of that perfection. In accepting our sexual energy we honor life as it really is. Sex is not bad or sinful as we have been taught to believe and it does not need to be hidden, denied and suppressed. Sex is the energy of life happening in us and we are that energy and whether we suppress it or express it, we are sexual beings. Sexual energy is part of us and it is moving through us all the time and moving us to the fulfillment of our own being. When we allow our sexual responses to flow we are allowing our self to be how we truly are.

Leaders of social institutions teach against sex because they were taught these same false ideas and were conditioned to hide and suppress their sexual responses and live in the illusion of these socially fabricated beliefs, just like the rest of us. We all grew up in the same socially fabricated illusions and we were indoctrinated into the same beliefs regarding sexual energy. No one grew up free of these socially fabricated illusions and conditioning that taught us to hide and suppress our sexual energy.

The suppression of our natural way of being, especially our sexuality, has been practiced for thousands of years and has been passed on to us, by everyone in our society. Suppression of our sexual energy has been taught for so long, it is generally accepted as the right way to be. Suppressing our energy has come to seem natural to us because we are all conditioned into this way of believing, thinking and acting and suppression has become the norm in society.

Every social group teaches some belief about how we should be but our beliefs are only concepts about life and like a chalk drawing of a bird they are only a picture of life and not the life they depict.

We are life happening, with all of our sexual and emotional energy the way it is and we can continue to suppress our real responses, as we have been trained to do or we can feel what we are really feeling, express ourselves fully and have the experiences that come to us from the open, honest and authentic expression of our real responses.

If we continue to suppress our real responses and continue to pretend other responses, we will continue feeling conflict within ourselves and in our relating with one another. When we hide and suppress our real responses, we are denying how we really are and interfering with the flow of our own energy and our own neurobiological system.

We can continue to believe the belief that our natural responses are bad, wrong, sinful or unacceptable and continue to suppress them or we can accept them as they are, realize this is the way we are designed to be and begin enjoying our lives fully.

If we continue in the mistaken belief that there is something wrong with us, we will continue to feel disturbed, unhappy, and unsatisfied with our real self and with our relationships. If we continue to deny our own responses and continue to suppress and hide them, we will continue feeling unfulfilled, incomplete and in conflict with our self and everyone else. If we continue to suppress our responses we will prevent ourselves from having authentic interactions and the pleasure of real connection and real intimacy with one another. If we continue suppressing rather than expressing what we are feeling we will continue feeling frustrated and unfulfilled. If we continue to maintain an image of how we think we should be and live in the illusions and pretenses of "how we should be" we will continue to be pretentious, superficial and hungry for real connection.

We may feel fear in making the decision to accept our self and express our self fully because it goes against everything we have been taught. Our fear is a responses to letting go of social beliefs and social conditioning to suppress our real responses and the possibility of being rejected. We were all raised with the same socially fabricated view of reality, the same conditioning and the same indoctrination into the same belief system that teaches us to hide and suppress ourselves. Our fear of rejection is a very deeply entrenched fear because we were punished and rejected to teach us to deny our self and following the beliefs of our culture.

We have been abused by parents, teachers, religious leaders, government leaders, wives, husbands, and friends to get us to suppress ourselves and adhere to these socially fabricated beliefs in exchange for acceptance and approval.

We do get rejected when we express our real responses openly and freely because we are living in a society that rejects us and teaches us to reject our self as a way of controlling us. We are rejected when we express our real responses because expression of our real responses is against the beliefs of our society. We are trained to hide, suppress and reject, so it is what we do to one another in our relationships. We are rejected when we express our real responses openly and we reject others when they express themselves openly. This is what we are trained to do when we do not follow the beliefs of our society.

CHAPTER 49

We Have Choice

———— ∞ ————

ACCEPTANCE OR REJECTION OF WHO we really are is our choice. We can focus on our real responses or we can focus on the beliefs about how we should be. What we focus on determines how we see our self, what we stimulate in our self and consequently, what we stimulate in our relationship with one another.

We are each created to be how we are and when we accept the way we are and express our real responses openly, freely and fully, we change the energy and dynamics of our own inner experience and our relationship with others.

CHAPTER 50

Focusing Our Attention

———— ⦾ ————

WE HAVE THE ABILITY TO focus our attention on whatever we want so we can focus our attention on our real responses or we can continue to focus on our socially fabricated beliefs and pretended responses. What we focus on stimulates our energy and our energy stimulates a resonant energy in others, creating our relational experience so when we focus on our belief about how we are supposed to be, others respond to our pretended expression.

It is our focus of attention that brings a particular experience into form. What we focus on creates our experience. This is the power of our focus of attention. Our ability to focus our attention gives us the ability to create any experience we want. When we change our focus from the socially fabricated illusion to our actual responses we change our energy, the way others react to us and therefore our relationships. When we focus on our actual responses, we are connected to who we really are, to our real energy and our experience of reality is influenced by our actual responses instead of the social illusion.

We have to train ourselves to focus our attention on our real responses after years of focusing on the conditioned ideas of our culture. We have to change our conditioned patterns of thought and behavior by changing our focus of attention from the socially fabricated beliefs to our actual responses. Focusing on our real sensations, feelings, thoughts and images allows us to respond from our own direct responses, as they really are. Focusing on our real responses allows us to tune in to our own experience of reality rather than focusing on the socially fabricated version about how we should be.

Like everyone else I learned to suppress my real responses and tried to be happy and fulfilled over top of my actual responses and in conflict with my real self. I focused on being good and right according to the beliefs I was taught, not realizing that I was causing my own conflict and unhappiness by suppressing my real responses. I didn't realize I was trained to suppress my responses and reject aspects of how I really am. I didn't realize I was trained to suppress my self and live within a social belief system that denies how we really are. I didn't know that I was born into a society that imposes a belief about how we should be, that isn't real.

My family was part of a society that believed we are all flawed, the socially fabricated illusions of what is wrong with us and how we should be. I didn't realize that I was born into a society that believes we wrong for being the way we are and instills this in everyone from the time we are born. I just wanted to be loved and accepted the way I am so I did my best to fit in and follow the rules.

Being real and expressing ourselves freely was not allowed so I learned to suppress, pretend, hide, deny and avoid, like everyone else, just to get along, be accepted and be okay with the people around me. I just wanted to be how I was, follow my truth, my reality, my way of being, express my actual responses and have my own experience of existence but expressing my self was not accepted or allowed so I learned to hide and suppress my responses, like everyone else.

Part of the training we all received was in arguing about right and wrong, good and bad, who was right and who was wrong. We were trained to argue and be in conflict with everyone around us.

I learned to argue and fight, just like everyone else, within the matrix of this social pattern. I have been arguing my whole life against the tyranny of the cultural beliefs that dominate the thinking of our society.

We live in a society that believes in suppressing feelings, sensations, and thoughts, hiding our bodies and "acting out" pretended responses, dictated by the prevailing social beliefs of our time. These pretended roles are determined by ideas about life inherited from our ancestors. Our ideas about reality however, are not the reality of how we really are.

Our beliefs are only conceptual pictures, describing and explaining reality. When we impose these conceptual ideas onto reality, by insisting that we fit ourselves into them, we interfere with the reality of how we really are. The imposition of beliefs on us is really the "tyranny of beliefs" and is interfering with our actual way of being and causing the conflict we are all experiencing. Suppressing our real responses and hiding our bodies to fit into these conceptual beliefs is a denial of reality and is the real sin of society and religion.

Focusing our attention is one of the most important skills we can learn and develop. It gives us the power to create what we really want and live in harmony with our real self and our actual responses to the world around us. Focusing our attention on what feels good, what feels resonant with us is our way of stimulating what we want into our experience of reality and is the way to create harmonious experiences in our reality. When we focus on what is resonant with us, we create harmonious vibrations in us and that stimulates harmonious experiences with others. Our whole being knows when something feels good and when it doesn't. Our biological system responds to what it likes and what it doesn't like. Our ability to notice what feels good is our guide to focusing our attention on what is right for us. When we focus on what feels good, our own neurobiological system is showing us what is best for us.

Even when we imagine something that feels good, we will feel positive, pleasurable sensations in us. This is our own biological system saying, "yes" to what we are imagining. When we focus our attention on what feels good to us, we stimulate positive energy in us and this positive energy causes positive experiences to happen with others and generally, in our lives.

Learning to shift our focus of attention from our patterns of negative thought and reactive behavior to what we like and enjoy requires a conscious effort because we have developed negative patterns of thought and behavior from the cultural beliefs that we are bad and wrong. We can change our experience when we change our focus and perception of our self to seeing our self as perfect manifestations of the energy of the Universe. When we feel disturbed it is because we are focused on the negative patterns of thought in our mind, criticizing and judging someone or something we don't like, especially our self.

Learning to shift our focus from criticism and judgment to acceptance creates a change in our inner energy and our outer experience. We must change our pattern of thought to create a different experience of reality for ourselves. When we learn to shift our focus to acceptance, our energy changes and with it our experience. What we give our attention to is creating our experience of life and when we change our focus we change our experience.

Learning to focus on our real responses connects us to our own personal experience and the guidance it provides, which allows us to focus on what feels good to us. We are each having our own responses and when we focus on them and follow them, we are our own guide to what is most beneficial to us.

CHAPTER 51

Our Authentic Responses

ACCEPTING OUR ACTUAL RESPONSES IS how we begin changing our experience of reality. Accepting our self is the way we give our self permission to be real and to express our real responses. By accepting them, as they are, we become conscious of them and allow them to be how they are and we learn to express our self freely.

This is very different from how we have been trained to think, believe, behave and express. Changing this socially developed pattern of rejecting ourselves to accepting ourselves is challenge but very rewarding because it opens the flow of our own energy and our interactions with others.

When we first meet, we feel excited and turned on to one another. We enjoy ourselves and our experience together until we get "plugged in" to the movie in our mind about how they should be or how we should be. Our feelings of love and excitement drown in a mental movie of what is right and wrong. Our natural responses of excitement and pleasure are lost in the movie of scripted roles as we try to change one another to fit into our movie versions of how we should be. We pretend to be how we think we should be, while we suppress and hide our real responses, until we can't stand the painful experience of mutual rejection and separation. Our lack of acceptance of our self and one another can never be cured with communication strategies because the real issue is our learned rejection of how we really are.

Switching from rejection to acceptance is a struggle because we are so conditioned to judge according to our learned ideas about right and wrong. Trying to make our experience of life feel better from within the socially fabricated movie of right/wrong doesn't really work because we respond to everyone from the limitations of this movie. Getting out of the movie starts with realizing we are living in a movie of socially fabricated ideas.

Our sensations, feelings, thoughts, images, fantasies, desires and wants are all there, continually happening in an ever changing flow of energy, no matter how much we suppress, hide or pretend to be the way we were taught we should be. Our responses are always happening in every moment and we can accept them or reject them.

Feeling something we have been taught is unacceptable brings up fear of being rejected by others. Our desire to be alone and to separate from others comes from a desire to feel what we are really feeling, without the fear of rejection. We are the way we are and yet our conditioning to suppress and hide our real responses and pretend some socially acceptable behavior takes over. We want to let go of the pretense and social illusions but we are afraid we will be rejected.

Breaking through the socially fabricated illusions in our mind and our own patterns of suppression and pretense is one of the most difficult things we can do. Our fear of being rejected by others is so conditioned into our thoughts, reactions and behavior, we must be very determined to break the trance of the social movie.

The solution is simple however it requires a clear decision, clear intention and determination. We are how we are, the way we were created to be by the Universe, whether we accept our self or not and we are feeling what we are feeling, whether we express it or not. The difference is that one is real and leads to our own fulfillment and the other is a fabricated social image that isn't real and makes us feel empty and unfulfilled.

This socially fabricated illusion is the world we all grew up in and we have all become a part of it but we don't have to continue living in it or living within it's restrictions. We don't like it and we have lost interest in our pretentious way of being and relating with one another.

We all want to be accepted for who we really are and we have to change our view and our patterns of thought and behavior to be who we really are and relate with others authentically, rather than playing our role in our shared social game.

We must create a different agreement if we are to release ourselves from the social illusions and relate honestly, openly and authentically. We must let go of the illusions completely to live in reality completely. We must stop suppressing our responses, stop pretending, stop hiding and stop denying our real self. As Werner Erhard said, "a transformed person is a person who can tell the truth and a transformed society is one in which the truth can be told".

CHAPTER 52

Changing Our View

———⊶⊷———

CHANGING OUR VIEW OF REALITY changes our experience of reality. When we change our perception we change our energy and therefor our relationship with everyone and everything. Changing our perception changes the energy we are emanating, which changes our interactions with others. When we perceive our self to be okay, to be perfect, as we are, we relax into who we really are and this changes our whole experience.

Changing our focus of attention is one of the most important skills we can learn and develop. When we develop our ability to shift our focus of attention, we can focus on what is really happening in us and respond in alignment with how we really are. Focusing our attention on what feels resonant with us allows us to guide ourselves into experiences that are truly aligned with us. Learning to focus our attention in our self presents us with the challenge of tuning into what feels right to us, what feels aligned with us and being able to focus on what we really want.

Although we are trained to focus on the socially fabricated conceptual ideas about how we should be that are not aligned with how we really are, we can change this and focus on what we are really feeling and thus be guided to what we really want. If our beliefs are not congruent with our own experience of reality, we can let go of focusing on the beliefs and shift our focus to what feels congruent and aligned with us. We have been taught to suppress and distrust our self, to deny our own experience and the perfection of our own being but we can change this by tuning in and focusing on our own responses, our own inner guidance system that is showing us through our own vibrations what is truly aligned with who we are and what is right for us.

CHAPTER 53

The Choice

———— ❦ ————

WE HAVE THE CHOICE TO accept ourselves as we really are or continue to adhere to the socially fabricated beliefs that tell us there is something wrong with us. We have the choice between being who we really are or pretending to be someone we are not, between expressing our actual responses or suppressing our real responses and acting out the pretended social behaviors we have learned. This is a choice we can and must make for ourselves.

The idea that there is something wrong with us is false. These are old beliefs about reality that are not real or true. Our sexuality, our emotions, our passions, our bodies are the perfect manifestation of the Universe, in human form. The way we are is the way we were created to be by the energy of the Universe. We are meant to enjoy life and to feel pleasure in all the ways that we do. We are naturally drawn to what feels good to us, to what feels pleasurable to us, to what excites us, to what we enjoy. Our sensations of pleasure move us into experiences that are the fulfillment of our being. Sensations of pleasure invigorate us in every cell of our bodies. Our sensations, feelings and images are aspects of being human and being alive in a physical body. We vibrate with all of these different energies and all of these energies are part of the reality of life, part of the reality of being human.

The socially driven illusion seems real so we argue over who's version of the illusion is good or bad or accurate. We argue in our attempts to impose our particular version of the social illusion onto one another and wonder why our relationships don't work. We think our view is "right" and that we are justified in imposing it onto everyone. The social illusion has as many guises as there are human beings. We each live in our own version of the social illusions and all of our conflicts come from trying to impose our beliefs on our self and on one another.

The only resolution to our conflict is to accept everyone and everything the way we really are. Acceptance of how we really are is the key to leaving the social illusions and learning to be with our actual way of being. Letting go of the belief that there is something wrong with us, allows us to leave the whole paradigm of right/wrong, blame, judgement, criticism, shame, hostility and rejection and this can only be done by accepting everyone and everything, just the way we are.

The conflict between our real responses and our learned beliefs can only be resolved by accepting them, every aspect of our humanness, including our physical bodies, our sexuality, sensations, feelings and our own individual experience.

Acceptance is the key. When we accept the way we really are we come into alignment with our self and we come into alignment with reality.

We are the way we are and we are having the only experience we can have, our own. Our energy and our responses are us happening and we can accept them, allow them, enjoy them and express them as they are or we can continue suppressing and rejecting our self and our responses, in homage to our social training and conditioning to believe in and live in the socially fabricated illusions that there is something wrong with us.

CHAPTER 54

Centering in Self

— ∞ —

CENTERING IN OUR SELF IS the act of focusing our attention in our self, in our own responses, in this energy that is happening in us, this energy that is us happening. Centering in our self shifts our focus of attention out of our socially indoctrinated mind movie and into our own direct experience of reality.

If we are playing in some socially fabricated belief about how we should be we are not being real and our relationships are nothing more than playing roles with one another and that doesn't lead to real connection or real intimacy. If we aren't being real our relationships aren't real either and we are just in a "fantasy bond" of two people acting out social roles.

When we are centered in our own energy, we are not in the movie of our learned social ideas about how we think we should be and we are able to express our real self, our real feelings, thoughts and sensations, openly and honestly and are able to relate authentically with one another. When we are centered in our own energy, in our own responses we are connected to our self and are able connect to one another and to the whole Universe around us.

The experience of fulfillment comes from being who we really are, from centering in our self, accepting our self and expressing all that that is, in each moment. When we are centered in our true self there is nothing to change or pretend because we are already being who and how we really are. Then we are what we have always been, a human being, one of the many differing forms of the energy of the universe.

CHAPTER 55

Happiness

—— ∞∞ ——

Happiness is an inner sensation of comfort and joy that happens when we accept our self. No one else can make us happy. We choose to be happy when we accept our self as we really are and enjoy our own experiences. We either accept our self or we do not. When we accept our self, we enjoy our self. When we reject our self, we feel bad and try to get someone else, to make us happy and then blame them, when they can't make us happy. Happiness does not come from outside us, from someone else accepting us or loving us. Happiness comes with acceptance of our self, as we really are and the enjoyment of our own experience, whatever it is.

When we are centered in our self and accepting our self, we feel relaxed having whatever experience we are having and we are fulfilled and satisfied with whatever that is. We can't get happiness from someone else. We can only get that sense of well being, comfort and enjoyment from accepting our self as we truly are.

When we try to get that sense of well being from someone else we are not centered in our own experience, so we are not fully present with our self or accepting what we are experiencing.

We may think we need someone else to be happy, so we pressure them to give us what we think we need from them and in the process cause pressure and stress in our relationship. We pressure them for a show of love, acceptance, approval or whatever we think will make us feel good. If they approve of us we may feel good for a while and that reinforces our notion that our well being is dependent on them instead of us. We think our sense of well being is dependent on them fulfilling our expectations and when our expectation is not being fulfilled, we feel let down, disappointed, angry, hurt, sad and insecure. When the other person isn't giving us what we want or think will make us happy or being the way we think they should be, we blame them and attack them to get them to give us what we expect from them and that causes conflict.

The illusion that we are not already perfect and that we can get happiness from someone else is the illusion most of us live in and believe in. We don't realize that our happiness and enjoyment of life is completely dependent on our acceptance of our self. Happiness only happens when we are centered in our self and accepting our self. When we center in our self and accept our self we are not trying to get it from someone else and we can then allow them to be how they really are. We are the source of our own experience of happiness. Happiness is a choice to accept our self and enjoy our own experience.

CHAPTER 56

Individual Creation of Experience

———— ❦ ————

OUR INDIVIDUAL EXPERIENCE OF REALITY is created by our focus of attention on a particular aspect of reality. When we are trained to focus our attention on something or in a particular way, we recreate that experience of reality over and over. If we perceive our self to be bad, wrong or flawed in some way, we will feel disturbed by how we are because that is the way our mind was taught to see ourselves. If we perceive our self to be perfect manifestations of the Universe then we accept our self, appreciate our self, and we will enjoy our own experience of life.

Our perception of life is stimulating our reactions to life, our experience of life and our relationship with life. We can't think we are bad and feel good about our self. When we perceive our self to be perfect the way we are, we feel positive energy in our self and in our relationship to life.

Perception is part of our neurobiological system that allows us to see and observe what we are encountering in life. Our thinking includes what we have learned and stored in our mind and is not the same as our ability to directly observe what is actually happening. Our mind has the ability to think about what we are observing but much of our thinking is the product of what we have been taught to think. Thinking is a process of assessing reality according to what we already know and when our thinking has been obscured by false ideas that do not accurately describe reality our observations are distorted. Deepak Chopra pointed out that we have approximately 65,000 thoughts a day but most of them are the same thoughts we had yesterday.

Assessment is a mental judgment of what we are looking at, based in our conceptual ideas about it. Assessing is a way of comparing what we are looking at, with our idea about it. This is observing, categorizing and making judgements about something rather than observing reality directly, and accepting it as it is. Assessing and categorizing something as good or bad, right or wrong, is looking at life through our conditioned ideas about reality, according to our learned understanding of it.

Accepting or rejecting someone or something stimulates our energy and therefor our interactions in the way we are relating to someone. If we accept our self the energy we stimulate is positive and this is the energy we feel in our self and the energy we bring to our interactions with others. Focusing on what we like, what we enjoy, what feels good, what feels natural and easy, creates that kind of experience for us. When our perception changes, our energy changes, our reactions change, our experiences change and our relationship with our self and others changes.

Our energy is determined by how we see our self, whether we accept or reject our self. If we judge, criticize, and reject some part of our self, our view and our energy is in conflict with how we really are and is creating conflict in us and in our relationships. When we don't accept our self we create negative energy in us and our negative energy stimulates a negative experience in us and with others. When we accept our self we relax into our own natural responses and we notice what pleases us, what we enjoy, what feels pleasurable and we follow that toward our own fulfillment. Accepting our self stimulates feelings of pleasure in us and we naturally move toward what pleases us. When we reject some part of our self we feel conflict and disturbance with that part of us and we bring that disturbance into our interactions with others, creating conflict in our relationships. Rejection of our self creates conflict. Acceptance of our self creates harmony.

Our social training teaches us to reject aspects of our self. We are trained to think there is something wrong with us, so we see ourselves in this negative way which stimulates negative energy in us. When we focus on what we don't like, what we are against and what we don't want, that is what we create in our experience. What we reject in others is what we are rejecting in our self. When we reject anything in our self we create negative energy in our self, we feel conflict and that conflict transfers to all of our relationships.

We expend a lot of energy arguing over what we don't like about one another and trying to change one another, not realizing that our negative energy is creating the conflict we are trying to resolve. When we think someone should be different then they are, we are not accepting them the way they are and we are creating the conflict between us and them. We blame one another, not realizing that our blaming is our rejection of them and that our rejection of them is creating the conflict we are experiencing.

Blaming others is a denial that we are the cause in our experience and that it is our rejection of some aspect of our self that is creating the problem. We are living in the illusion of right and wrong and we blame others for the negative experience that we are creating. We think the other person is the problem and deny that it is our negative energy that is creating the problem.

We all know how this kind of thinking can take over and consume us and our whole experience of reality. When we think someone is wrong, we believe our own thoughts and our disapproval is expressed in our energy, in every word we speak, in our attitude and our behavior. We project our own self rejection and think they are wrong for being the way they are and we justify our negativity by blaming our feelings on them. We blame them for our rejection of them.

When we are in this socially fabricated movie of right and wrong we can't see that the conflict we are experiencing is being caused by our rejection our self and them. Our inability to accept our self gets projected onto others and creates a whole chain of negative energy and reactions that becomes our pattern of thought, energy and behavior.

When we focus on our ideas about how someone should be, we are lost in our socially fabricated movie and we are the one not accepting the reality of how they really are. We are rejecting them and we think our rejection is being caused by them.

Our judgment, blame and rejection is a reflection of the socially fabricated movie into which we were born and indoctrinated and our belief that there is something wrong with everyone. We are all so conditioned into the social movie of right/wrong we actually believe we are justified in judging, blaming and rejecting others.

We criticize, judge, blame and send negative energy at one another, with remarks, attitudes, disapproving looks and rejection in all the many forms. We reject our self for being the way we are and we project these judgements onto everyone else and we show them in every way we can that they aren't okay and are the problem in our life. We don't accept our self or anyone else and we don't take responsibility for our judgement or our rejection of them.

When we accept our self and others, as we really are, there is no problem and there is no conflict. We are exactly how we are, how we are designed to be and when we get this simple truth, we come into harmony with our self and with everyone else, as well. When we accept how we are, we also accept others the way they are and we relax into life, as it is.

CHAPTER 57

Energy

———— ✸✸ ————

EVERYTHING IS ENERGY. ENERGY IS everything. The whole Universe is energy, in some form or another. We are the energy of the Universe and we are all having our own energetic responses to the energy that is in us and all around us. Our thoughts, sensations and feelings are our energetic responses to life that are guiding us to what is right for us, in harmony with us and our energy is felt by others and stimulates our interactions with others. We are the energy of the Universe in human form and our whole energetic system and our whole physical system is designed to be exactly the way it is and it is responding to the universe around us and guiding us through our experiences.

Our focus of attention stimulates our energy in the form of sensations and emotional responses. Our ideas about life are like movies in our mind that stimulate our energy and cause us to respond with sensations and emotions like they do when we are watching a movie. We react to our own mind movie the way we react to a movie at the theater. Changing our focus of attention is like watching a different movie and changing the movie we are watching, changes our experience.

By tuning in to our own feelings we can focus on what is most resonant with us, what pleases us and what we are drawn toward. When something feels pleasurable this is a response of resonance. We are naturally attracted to anything that feels good, because pleasurable sensations are positive forms of energy, a form of resonance that moves us toward what is in harmony with us. When we are centered in our own responses, they guide us to what is right for us, what is in harmony with us. Tuning in to what feels good stimulates our energy in a pleasurable way, moving us toward what is most beneficial for us. We only have to tune into our own positive feelings of resonance to guide ourselves to what is perfect for us.

To do this we have to let go of the socially fabricated movie in our mind of how we should be and tune into our own natural energetic responses. We have to accept our self, just the way we are, feel our own responses and follow our own sensations and feelings to where they are guiding us. When we focus on our own energy we are centered in our own experience instead of the cultural beliefs.

We are a living, organic, neurobiological form of life happening and we are exactly the way we were designed to be and when we accept how we are and relax into our own sensations and feelings we relax into our real self and we can allow ourselves to happen naturally.

CHAPTER 58

Being Alone

—— ⚬⚬⚬ ——

BEING ALONE CAN BE HELPFUL in learning to center in our self and be aware of our own moment to moment responses that are happening in us. Being alone allows us a little distance from others who have similar conditioning and this can support us in freeing ourselves from the reinforcement of similar patterns in others.

Most of us are traumatized very early from being rejected by our families and the society around us, so we need time and space to open to our own individual feelings and sensations that have been held in for our whole lives. Being alone allows us time to tune into our own energy and become familiar with our own responses so we can learn to center in them, allow them, feel them fully and accept them.

We feel nervous and uncomfortable with our own feelings and sensations because we were taught to feel bad about them, suppress them and hide them, so at first, allowing ourselves to feel them stimulates feelings of discomfort. By centering in our feelings and sensations and accepting them as they arise, we learn to relax into them and allow them to be how they are.

Being alone helps us to tune into what we are feeling without the fear of others seeing us and rejecting us. Gradually we began to be able to center in our sensations and feelings and stay with what we are feeling without the fear of rejection and the distraction of others and our mutual patterns of hiding and suppressing.

It takes time to do this but eventually we are able to stay centered and focused on our feelings and sensations and we can allow them to flow freely through us. Eventually, we are able to feel our responses as they are happening, even with the discomfort that comes up at the same time. It helps to take long deep breaths as we focus on our feelings, sensations and thoughts, allowing the energy of fear and anxiety to be released from our body and allowing us to relax.

We spend our lives hiding and suppressing our real responses and acting out socially pretended roles that we learned growing up in our society. Being alone gives us some freedom from the pressure of possible criticisms and judgments, as well as some distance from the social patterns of thought and behavior of others.

Every feeling, sensation and thought will come up and pass through our body and mind; fear, anxiety, shame, guilt, anger, sadness, love and sexuality, in the process of allowing ourselves to feel what we are really feeling. Everything that is in us arises along with our fear of allowing ourselves to see and feel whatever is coming up for us.

We are afraid of being how we really are, with all of our real feelings, sensations, thoughts, and fantasies, all the stuff we have learned to suppress around others, so being alone allows our real feelings, sensations and thoughts to arise more freely. When we are alone we learn to center in our self, in our own responses and we learn to accept our real responses, as they are flowing through us. Being alone allows us to shift our focus from the socially fabricated movie in our head, into our actual responses, as they are happening.

I few years ago I went to a cabin, deep in the woods to be alone and face my own feelings and thoughts. At first I paced like a cat in a cage, moving, cleaning, organizing, reading, writing, walking, running, stretching, breathing, doing yoga, fantasizing and watching my own mind and body going through all kinds of thoughts, feelings and sensations. In the beginning I was filled with anxiety with what was coming up.

Everything I had been suppressing came up and moved through me like so much energy that had been blocked behind a wall of suppression and inhibition. Initially, I couldn't relax so I paced and distracted my self with cleaning, fixing things and tying to reduce the intensity of my own energy. As I stayed with my own energy, my emotions and sensations and thoughts I was more able to allow them to flow more freely, without blocking them. I was alone and there was no one to reject or criticize me so over a couple months I began to relax into my responses and was able to feel them and observe them as they moved through me. Eventually I was able to feel my feelings and sensations fully and was able to express my responses more openly, honestly and freely with words and sounds.

Accepting the feelings and sensation that were moving in me and through me allowed me to express them and this was a process of retraining my own neurobiological system to flow and express more freely. I was learning how to feel what I was really feeling and be aware of my real feelings and sensations by centering in my actual responses and allowing my self to feel them and express them.

In the process of learning to focus on my actual sensations and feelings I also was able to express them more fully, freely and authentically. I was learning to focus on and feel my real responses and be aware of them to a point of acceptance and allowance of what was actually moving through me. It was easier to accept and allow my real responses to flow when I wasn't around others, in the middle of the socially driven movie about what is and isn't acceptable to feel and think.

I felt nervous and anxious initially and in time I realized that my feelings of nervousness and anxiety were part of my learned shame, discomfort and rejection of my own responses. I was going through the process of letting go of my learned suppression and I realized that my disturbance with my own responses was part of my learned rejection.

This is why it is so difficult for us to feel our actual responses or express them authentically and why changing our patterns of hiding and suppressing requires that we focus our attention on the sensations and feelings that are moving in us. We must have a strong intention to get out of our head, out of our mind movie and feel our actual responses and accept them, in order to center in them, tune into them and relax into what we are really experiencing.

Tuning into our real responses is an intense experience of feeling our actual feelings of fear, anger, sadness, love, sexuality, happiness, pain, pleasure, grief, loneliness, craziness, brilliance and creativity that are all part of our neurobiological system continuously moving energy in us and through us.

When we are feeling our own responses fully, we feel invigorated with our own energy and we are guided by our own energy impeccably. We are the only one having our experience and we are the only one who can tune into it, feel it, express it and be guided by it. Our own neurobiological system is extraordinary and functions perfectly when we allow it to flow freely.

Our energy is continuously responding to the world around us because we are all energy in differing forms and we are having our own individual experience of this energetic reality while interacting with one another.

The end of our conflict can only come with accepting ourselves completely; our body, thoughts, emotions and sensations, in all the ways they are happening in us. We have to accept all of what is moving through us to feel okay with our self as we really are. When we accept our own anger, fear, sadness, love, sexuality, thoughts and images, we are accepting our humanness as it really is.

All of our responses are a natural part of being human and they are happening in us with or without our consent or opinion. How we respond to our own feelings and sensations makes a difference in how we relate to our self and the world around us. We are human beings with feelings, sensations and thoughts and when we accept them and allow them to flow freely, we relax into them and can enjoy all of our experiences.

All of our thoughts, feelings, sensations, images, visions and fantasies can flow through us freely when we are not hiding, suppressing and inhibiting them. We are energy in physical form and every cell of our body, every molecule of our energy is us happening. We are life happening in human form with feelings, sensations and thoughts that are all aspects of our neurobiological system. We are life happening and every part of our being is life happening, including our penis, vagina, clitoris, anus, nipples, lips, thoughts, feelings, sensations, fantasies, visions and images. All of these aspects are part of the flow of our own energy, the energy of the Universe, in human form. We are life happening exactly the way we are and we are meant to be exactly the way we are and when we accept ourselves the way we are, we can enjoy who we are and how we are and we can enjoy all of life.

The socially established limitations on what we are allowed to feel, think and express is part of our social training, so having a space in which to be real and to feel what we are really sensing, feeling and thinking and having the freedom to express all of it is essential to changing the patterns of hiding, suppressing and contracting against our own natural way of being.

For me to get free and begin to relax into my self, into my own responses and begin to express my self fully and freely, I needed a few months. I had strong patterns of suppressing and contracting against my feelings and thoughts so it took me awhile to get use to feeling my real responses and allowing my self to express them.

As we accept our own responses, our inner conflicts resolve and we also begin to allow everyone else to be how they are, which resolves much of our relational conflicts. Our inner conflicts dissolve naturally as we accept our real responses and our conflicts with others resolve because we are able to accept them as well.

Centering in our responses shifts our focus away from our socially driven games with others and we are guided by our actual responses to and with others. When we finally focus in our own experience, we begin living our own life authentically, from our own responses, our own inner guidance and we begin flowing and enjoying our own experience, whatever it is. In addition, we begin to accept others and let them be the way they really are, without our criticisms and judgements of them. Focusing in our own responses creates an awareness in us that allows others to have their own responses without our interference and this creates harmonious energy and feelings in our relationships. Focusing in our own responses relaxes us into our true self and we begin to emanate positive and relaxed energy into our relationships. When we are okay with our self, we are also okay with others.

Expressing our responses openly and honestly happens naturally when we accept our energy and simply allow our feelings and sensations to be how they are. Our sensations, feelings and thoughts are all happen, naturally, as part of us happening, so accepting them, allowing them and expressing them frees us from the patterns of hiding, suppressing and contracting against them.

Expressing our self with sounds, words, and actions is natural to all of life. Talking, smiling, looking, touching, smelling, kissing, hugging and sexing are all natural expressions of our real responses that are always moving in us and flowing through us. Fantasies, desires, wants and needs arise in us when we allow them to flow freely and allow them to express.

Our real life begins when we accept our real self completely and allow our real responses to move freely through us.
Accepting our responses fully and completely allows us to flow
freely energetically and we begin to feel comfortable with our
responses and our whole neurobiological system opens and begins to flow freely. Crying, laughing, breathing, groaning, sigh-
ing, grinning, touching, tasting, smelling, all happens naturally
and continuously when we allow our responses to flow freely.
When we allow our responses to flow freely, our whole being begins to open and our energy flows naturally and spontaneously
and then we are the flowing energy of the Universe, in human
form.

CHAPTER 59

Sex

———— ◦◦◦ ————

SEX IS A NATURAL PART of life, of being human, of being how we are designed to be, with all of our sexual parts, filled with sensations of pleasure so we will come together sexually. Sexual sensations are pleasurable so they will stimulate in us a desire to be sexual. All of life is sexual. All of life comes from sexual activity. Our sexual responses are natural and being sexual is natural. Sexual pleasure creates some of the most pleasurable sensations we can experience and these intense sensations of pleasure brings us together to fulfill our desire for pleasure, connection and is natures way of creating new life.

Pleasure feels good and even with all the false beliefs that sex is bad or sinful, we can't stop ourselves from being sexual because it is what we are designed to do. Sexual pleasure is a natural part of our being, life fulfilling life, through sexual pleasure.

Desire is a word we use to refer to the sensations in our body and images in our mind, when we want sexual pleasure. Desire is an aspect of our neurobiological system that drives us to our own sexual activity and fulfillment. When we feel desire our sexual energy is driving us to be sexual for our own fulfillment, health, well being, vitality and aliveness. Our sensations of pleasure are guiding us toward our own fulfillment and to the fulfillment of life. We are life happening in human form and we are here to experience life and all of the pleasures of life, including the pleasures of being sexual.

The Universe created us with feelings and sensations, in order for us to feel them and follow them to our own fulfillment and when we are sexual our neurobiological system is working perfectly. We are human beings and we are here to be how we are designed to be and being sexual is part of our design.

We are the Universe happening in the form of a human being and our life as human beings includes our physical bodies with all the emotional and sexual energy we feel in our whole body including our vagina, penis, breasts, nipples and anus. We are living, breathing, manifestations of the Universe, with feelings, sensations and thoughts flowing through us that are stimulating us into our interactions with everyone and everything we encounter.

Pleasure is a natural neurobiological response to anything we like, whether it is sexual pleasure or laughter or the pleasure of seeing something beautiful, we respond naturally with pleasurable sensations. Pleasure is our natural response to whatever pleases us, to what we like, what we enjoy, what feels good. Pleasure is our own neurobiological system signaling us that something is good for us. We feel pleasure with our whole body, with all of our senses, our body vibrates with pleasure and we expresses these sensations with sounds and movement, as these feelings of pleasure flow through us. We ooh, ahh, groan, grunt, gurgle, giggle, laugh, sigh and purr when we feel sensations of pleasure moving through us in response to someone or something that feels good to us. "Ooh, ahh, mmm, that feels so good, that smells so good, that tastes so good". Pleasurable sensations are stimulated in us anytime anything feels good to us.

We have been taught to think that pleasure is bad and yet we all enjoy the pleasurable sensations moving through us when we like something, whether its the smell of delicious food or getting turned on and having sexual pleasure in all of it's many forms. We all enjoy pleasure in any form, whether it comes in the form of laughter, happiness or an orgasm. Pleasure is a natural part of our neurobiological system, letting us know something is good for us.

CHAPTER 60

The Universe

———— ⬡ ————

THE UNIVERSE IS PURE ENERGY and we are one form of this energy among many the many different forms in the Universe. Einstein said, " energy is mass and mass is energy and nothing is ever created or destroyed, it is simply changing form."

We can call the energy of the Universe, God, Great Spirit, Pali, Cali, Krishna, Chita, Allah, Yahweh or Elokim, but regardless of what we call it, we are, everyone and everything is, some form of this energy. We make up words to refer to this energy but this energy is what it is, regardless of what we call it. We make up the words we use but the energy of the Universe is the way it is in all these different forms and our words are only symbols referring to this energy.

We may never be able to fully understand or explain the Universe to ourselves or have the understanding we want but the fact is, we are here in physical human form, one unique form, an integral part of the Universe, just the way we are.

Universe by definition, means one verse. Universe is a word that refers to the whole thing, everything, all of it, including us. We are this energy and this energy is us. This energy, which is the Universe, is happening in form and we, along with everyone and everything else, are this happening.

We argue over who's word, description or explanation is right but our ideas and opinions are only descriptions and explanations. We've been killing one another for all of recorded history over who's explanation and description is right and we try to impose our particular ideas, as if our explanations are real. We are arguing over our different beliefs, descriptions and explanations. We forget that our descriptions are only descriptions and our explanations are only explanations. The Universe is the way it is and we are all part of the energy of the Universe in human form, regardless of our beliefs, descriptions, and explanations about it.

We have been living in an illusion that our beliefs are reality, when they are merely our conceptual ideas about reality. A belief is only a concept about reality. Reality is what is. Reality is how we really are. Our beliefs, descriptions and explanations are nothing more then conceptual ideas, put into words. Our beliefs are not reality. Life the way it is is reality and that includes us.

We say that our beliefs come from God and are therefor, unquestionable. We believe that our particular belief about reality, about life, about being human is given by God and is therefor unquestionable but we are the ones making up these beliefs.

Reality is what is. Life itself, as it is, is the only truth, the only reality. How we really are is the only truth. We pretend to ourselves that our beliefs come from God but this is our way of convincing others that our beliefs are right. Beliefs are made up by human beings trying to explain reality but our explanations are not reality, as it actually is.

God is a word that refers to the energy of the Universe but the word God is not the reality of this energy. Reality is life, as it is, including our feelings, sensations and our bodies. Words are just words. We make up words to talk about reality but our words are not reality. They are like chalk drawings, only a picture of something. Our beliefs, descriptions, and explanations are just words, conceptual ideas about reality and not reality, as it is.

CHAPTER 61

We Are Life Happening

———— ∞ ————

WE ARE LIFE HAPPENING, JUST as we are and just as we are meant to be. We are perfect in every way. Every sensation, feeling, image and body part is us happening, our whole being, being life, responding as life, with life, to life. We are life happening. Our whole way of being, our bodies, our feelings, our sensations, our responses do not conform to any conceptual belief. Our ideas and beliefs are like chalk drawings of a bird. They are not real, merely pictures of reality. They are not life happening, as it really is. When we tune into our self, to our energy, our real responses and experience our self fully, we are having our own direct experience of reality and have the one thing that can bring us fulfillment and happiness and that is "our real self". We have to accept the life that we are and all the responses that are part of being human.

We are life happening, with all the sensations, feelings and thoughts that are moving through us, in every moment. Our interactions with life, with one another are the expression of our responses to life. We are life in human form happening naturally, as we are created to be and we are beyond any belief that we may have about it. We are the energy of the Universe happening in human form prior to and regardless of our beliefs about it.

When we allow our self to be how we really are, we aren't forcing or resisting anything. Our responses are just happening. Sexual responses, emotional responses are all part of being human beings and having our natural responses to life. Sex is a natural part of being human, part of life happening, part of the Universe happening, life responding to life. When we accept and allow every part of us to be how it is, we respond perfectly in our actions and interactions with one another.

We are conditioned to suppress our sexual responses especially and to pretend we are not having sexual responses when we are having them. We are taught to hide our sexual responses and pretend something else. We are taught to pretend not to be sexual in order to conform to the way our group believes we should be, according to these beliefs about how we "should be" which are not the reality of how we really are. We pretend to hide what we are really experiencing whether it's sexual or emotional. We've been taught to deny all of our natural responses in favor of these socially learned roles that come out of our conceptual ideas about "how we should be". The truth is that we are all emotional and sexual beings and we are attracted to one another energetically, emotionally and sexually because all of our responses bring us together in close, physical, intimate relationship which is something we all want. We are social beings and we all want to be loved and accepted physically, emotionally and sexually.

CHAPTER 62

Social Beings

———∞∞∞———

WE ARE SOCIAL BEINGS AND we want to maintain positive relationships with others in our group, so we struggle with expressing our real responses because they are not always accepted by others in our society, especially if our responses are sexual and we don't want to be rejected so we hide and suppress what we are feeling and thinking. We have all been indoctrinated into these same beliefs so we all learn to suppress our emotional and sexual responses to fit in and be accepted by others.

Herein lies the challenge for each of us, to be who we really are, to be human, in a world of illusion. Can we let go of these socially fabricated beliefs about how we should be and just be how we really are? Can we accept our own feelings, sensations and individual thoughts and express ourselves openly, honestly, fully and freely? Can we let go of these socially fabricated conceptual illusions and recognize that we are perfect manifestations of the Universe, just as we are? Can we change our focus from these conceptual ideas about how think we should be and accept ourselves as we really are? Can we accept our self and others the way we really are, including our bodies, our emotions and our sexuality?

Social groups try to control their members through teaching, conditioning, and indoctrination. Repeating the same things over and over until these beliefs are drummed into our minds. We learn these conceptual views and learn to think and see them in our mind, as if they are real and then we tell others these beliefs and play a role in this tyranny of beliefs over reality. We justify our oppression and suppression of how we really are because we have come to believe in the socially fabricated illusions and reject the reality of how we really are.

We have a choice and we are always choosing between the socially fabricated illusions and being who we really are, human beings living in a world of illusion.

CHAPTER 63

Following Our Energy

———— ⁊⁊ɕ ————

WE ARE THE ENERGY OF the Universe in human form. The word Universe means one whole verse, everything, the Whole, all of it and we are part of this everything. The Universe is manifesting as energy and form and we are part of this energy and form. We are the way we are by the design of the Universe and we are just one perfect form of the infinite forms of the Universe.

We use the word God to refer to the energy of the Universe. We are the energy of the Universe so we are the energy of God. Universe and God are words we use to refer to this energy. Words like God and Universe are different words for the same thing. Everyone and everything in the Universe is the Universe in some particular form. Everyone and everything is the physical manifestation of this energy of the Universe some call God, the mass that is energy, the energy that is mass, in human form. We are this energy and this energy is us, in the form of a human being.

When teachers have said that God is within us, they meant exactly that. We are made of this energy of the Universe that some call God. The awareness that we are the manifestation of God has not registered fully in our awareness as a whole, as a collective but the awareness that we are the perfect manifestation is coming into human awareness. God is simply a word referring to the energy of the Universe in all of it's various forms, including us. We are this energy and we are part of this energy, one form of this energy, this everything we call the Universe and this means that we are part of the everything that we call God. In other words we are the energy of the Universe. We are God.

We make up stories about how God created the Universe and how God created us but these are only stories that human beings made up to explain something they didn't fully understand. like thinking the world is flat or that the sun revolves around the earth. We get lost in the stories and forget that they are just stories and that we are the energy of the Universe that is manifesting in form, human beings. We are the physical manifestation of the Universe and whether we call it God or Allah or Yahweh or Shiva or Energy, we are this energy we are referring to. This energy is the form and substance of existence.

We are the energy and form of the Universe and it doesn't matter whether we call this energy God or Universe. We are this energy and when we understand this simple fact and accept ourselves as we are, our own experience of reality as the Universe happening, we will begin letting go into the experience and flowing more easily with this energy that we are.

When we see that we are the perfect manifestation of the Universe we can begin accepting and allowing our self to be how we are and begin our life, enjoying our self and enjoying one another, the way we are. When accept our self as we are in all our different forms of the energy of the Universe, we can relax and be in harmony with all of it. We are all the chosen ones. No one is more chosen than anyone else. We are all here, manifesting in form and that means we are all a form of God manifesting in human form.

All of our ideas about God being in heaven, hovering like some nebula, controlling us and punishing us, are simply misperceptions about reality. These beliefs are just stories made up by our ancestors who were trying to explain the unfathomable mystery of reality. We all have ideas about reality that are our own neurobiological system trying to understand and explain the unfathomable nature of the Universe. Ideas and beliefs are the accumulated thoughts of human beings trying to understand so we could guide ourselves through life, but these ideas and beliefs are only a mental picture, a conceptual idea about life and not life as it is.

Our ancestors did their best to understand the Universe because they wanted to be in harmony with it so they could survive and prosper and hand this knowledge and skills onto their children. We are doing the very same thing in this moment using stories to explain existence, as best we can, just like our ancestors did but these stories are not the reality of our actual experience and way of being. The mistake we are making is the same mistake our ancestors made in thinking that our conceptual ideas and beliefs are the reality of existence itself.

When we believe our conceptual ideas are reality, we are making this same mistake and we are preventing ourselves from simply being who and how we are and accepting our own individual experience. In the process we lose our own awareness of what is actually happening in us in the moment. When we lose an awareness of what we are experiencing we are in the movie in our mind rather that tuned into our own experience in the moment.

When we teach our beliefs as "the truth" we are missing the mark in misunderstanding what is actually happening and imposing these illusions of our mind onto the experience we are having. When we pass beliefs and ideas on to the next generation as if they are the truth, we are teaching them to live in the conceptual illusions of their minds and teaching them to miss their actual experience.

We all have thoughts, feelings, sensations, images, fantasies, visions and a body that functions the way it is designed to function and we do not function according to our beliefs. We function the way we are created to function by the energy of the Universe. We are the energy of the Universe happening in human form and we are perfect exactly the way we are and our beliefs are simply conceptual pictures in our minds.

When we see that our beliefs are just pictures of reality, meant to give us understanding and guidance we can make this distinction between what is just an idea, a belief, a picture about reality and not reality as it is, not the reality of our actual experience or way of being.

We are the reality of the Universe happening in human form and we are perfect exactly the way we are. We are the Universe happening in human form, physically, emotionally, mentally, and energetically. Every impulse, every thought, every sensation, every feeling we have is a neurobiological response to what is happening and a message from the energy that is happening in us, guiding us toward or away from what is around us. Our responses are messages from our own neurobiological system, guiding us and showing us what resonates with us, what will ful-fill us and support us in living fully and surviving successfully. Our whole neurobiological system is designed to guide us to the fulfillment of our own wants, needs and desires.

The stories and beliefs of our ancestors came from human beings trying to understand and explain reality. Their stories about creation were attempts to explain this unseen energy of the Universe out of which everything is manifesting but they were after all just stories attempting to explain things they did not fully understand.

When we see that we are a manifestation of the energy of the Universe and accept ourselves as we are and allow our self to be the way we are, the way the energy of the Universe is manifest-ing in the form of a human being, we can accept ourselves, our form and energetic responses and we can be present with the reality that is actually happening in us, as it is.

CHAPTER 64

Images in Our mind

——— ∞∞∞ ———

IMAGES APPEAR IN OUR MIND of what we want and desire, stimulating energy in the form of sensations and emotional responses that are our responses to our own images. Images, fantasies, thoughts and visions are our minds way of seeing beyond present reality to possible solutions to our needs, wants and desires. Images appearing in our mind is the way our own neurobiological system is responding to some need, want or desire.

When we are trained to focus on conceptual ideas and beliefs they become more prominent than our actual responses and like when we are watching a movie we have responses, feelings and sensations in response to the movie we are watching. Our sensations and feelings can be stimulated by our actual responses or to the movie playing in our mind. If we see this distinction we can shift our attention from the movie in our mind to our actual responses that are happening in us.

When we believe that our learned conceptual beliefs about reality are real, we are responding to a conceptual movie in our mind rather than to what is actually happening in the moment. When we are living in the movie in our mind we deny our actual responses and this creates conflict between our real responses and the movie in our mind.

We live in a world that believes in the illusions of the conceptual mind and these illusion are a contradiction to our actual responses and this creates all the conflict and struggle in us. As long as we believe in the illusions of our society we will be in conflict with our self, others and reality as it is. If we do not accept our actual responses, we are unable to tune into them or allow them to guide us.

We may get rejected by people who believe in the socially fabricated ideas about how we should be but if we free ourselves from the illusions of our culture we are free to be who we really are, free to express ourselves fully and free to live our lives fully. We either live in these socially fabricated illusions of our society or we let go of them, center in our own experience and have our own experience of reality, as it is for us.

Visions are part of our neurobiological system, showing us images of possible realities that we can create for our own fulfillment. Visions come into our awareness, showing us what we want for the fulfillment of our own life. We are continuously seeing what we want in the form of images and visions and it is always guiding us toward the fulfillment of our own life. We are life and life is a continual movement of energy that is spontaneous, continuous and interactive with everyone and everything. Visions are our way of seeing what might be and guiding ourselves and our own focus of attention through the changing experiences of our lives.

We feel, sense, see and respond with sensations, feelings and images that are all part of our neurobiological response mechanism, guiding us toward the fulfillment of our needs, wants and desires. When we tune in to our own energy, our own responses, our feelings, sensations and images they guide us toward the fulfillment of our own life

Tuning into our own responses is tuning into our own inner guidance system and allowing ourselves to see which way to go, what to do and how to respond. Knowing what to do is a matter of tuning in to our own inner responses and allowing them to guide us. Our system is designed to guide itself and our job is to tune in to our own responses and follow our own guidance. We know when something feels good to us and when it doesn't. We feel it, we sense it and it expresses as feelings, sensations, images, thoughts and visions. These are all forms of our own integrated neurobiological energy system, responding and showing us the way to our own fulfillment. All we have to do is tune in and follow the guidance our own responses are giving us.

We have been taught to think we can't trust our ability to tune in and know what our own responses are showing us and guiding us toward but as we develop our ability to tune into what we are feeling and sensing, we gain confidence in our own neurobiological feedback system. We just have to tune in, center in our own responses, allow ourselves to feel them and follow them to what they are showing us. The more we do it the easier it is to do it.

CHAPTER 65

Pleasure

———— ∞ ————

PLEASURABLE SENSATIONS ARE GUIDING US to what is most beneficial for us, what we want, need and desire for our own fulfillment. Pleasure is a sensation produced by our own neurobiological system, exciting us and moving us to action and guiding us to the fulfillment of our being.

Pleasure is an aspect of neurobiological system that supports our health and well being by making us feel good and vibrate with life energy, vital energy in the form of pleasurable sensations that can be stimulated with singing, dancing, talking, tasting, touching, seeing, smelling, hearing. Pleasurable sensations feel good to us because they are good for us. Pleasurable sensations are positive responses to life, our own systems way of guiding us to what is healthy for us, what is right for us, what feels good to us, what enlivens us and fulfills us. Pleasurable sensations energize us by stimulating our energy and giving us the vital energy to be healthy, happy and fulfilled.

The sensations of pleasure is a natural part of our neurobiological design, guiding us to experiences that are good for us. We are designed to feel pleasure for our own health and well being and when we feel pleasure, when we are enjoying our self we are being healthy, happy and good. When we allow our self to feel pleasurable sensations we are in the flow of life and we are being guided by our own system to what is naturally good for us and we are doing what is healthy for us and living the way we are meant to live and the way we were designed to live.

Sexual pleasure is one of the most natural pleasures for all of us and one of the most wonderful pleasures that we can experience and enjoy.

CHAPTER 66

Acceptance

———— ✐ ————

ALL OF OUR "CONDITIONS FOR acceptance" are just forms of rejection. We have learned concepts about what is and what is not acceptable so we reject aspects of how we are based on these socially fabricated beliefs about what is not acceptable.

We learn to argue over who is right and who is wrong because of our different views of reality and we try to impose our version of reality on others because we do not accept some part of reality, as it is, some part of our self, some part of them. We have been trained to think there is some particular way to be, think or act and we try to impose these socially fabricated beliefs on everyone.

Acceptance is not an act of believing some belief about life, about how it should be. Acceptance is allowing life to be the way it is, allowing our self to be how we are and allowing others to be how they are. When we accept how we are, we are accepting how the Universe is.

The only resolution to the conflict we feel is acceptance. If I am arguing with you about how you are I am not accepting reality as it is. If I am not accepting how I am or how you are, I am arguing with reality. Acceptance is not argument and does not involve argument or being against someone. If we are arguing we are not accepting some part of reality, as it is, whether it is some part of our self or some part of someone else.

We are either accepting or rejecting some part of life. We are either in acceptance and harmony or in rejection and disturbance. We are either in peace or we are in conflict, depending on whether we are accepting or rejecting our self or someone else. Acceptance stimulates harmony and rejection stimulates conflict. We are always doing one or the other. We are creating our own experience and the interactions we are having with others by whether we are accepting or rejecting some part of our self or them.

Harmony is an inside job and so is disturbance. We create our own harmony and happiness when we accept and we create our own conflict and suffering when we reject. When we accept everyone and everything, as it is, we stimulate harmony in our self and in our interactions with others. We are always stimulating either conflict or harmony, by whether we are accepting or rejecting. Acceptance or rejection is the choice we are making and this choice is creating our experience. Acceptance or rejection is a choice we are always making and is the only choice that makes a real difference in how we live our life. Acceptance creates harmony. Rejection creates conflict.

If we want joy, happiness, peace, harmony and pleasure, we have to accept the way we are and the way everyone else is. There is no other cure for the conflict and struggle we are all in with our self and one another. There is no other thing that can be done or action that must be taken to change our lives. There is no argument to be won or person to blame. We are all responsible for whether we accept or reject someone or some part of life. We are also responsible for changing our own thinking and behavior from rejection to acceptance of our self and others.

We are either accepting or rejecting. Our training is to reject how we are and we have learned to play our role in the socially fabricated view of reality by not accepting our self or others and not show our actual responses, which is a socially learned rejection of our self. We can reject our self and play out our social role or we can accept our self and be how we really are. There is a world of difference between living according to the social beliefs which teaches us to judge and reject our self and others and begin accepting our self and others as we really are.

Rejection of our self, as we are, is the cause of all the conflicts we are having and acceptance is the resolution. When we do not accept our self or someone else, we are rejecting the Universe and reality, as it is.

We have to let go of our social training to that taught us to reject, judge, criticize, suppress, oppress and impose these false and limiting ideas of "how we should be" if we want our lives to be fully alive and free and exciting. Acceptance is the resolution to all the conflicts we feel inside and all the conflict we are creating in our relationships.

When we accept our self, we realize that our sensations, our feelings, our thoughts, are just different forms of the energy of life, moving through us and they are all part of the experience of being a human being. This energy moving through us, is us, in the form of sensations, feelings, thoughts. We are physical manifestations of the energy of the Universe happening, in human form and we are the way we are by Universal design. When we realize this, accept this and allow this, we allow our energy to open and vibrate with the full energy of life. When we accept our self in all the ways that we are happening, we relax into our self, into our own responses and we feel the pure pleasure of being.

There is nothing we need to do to change, fix or improve our self because we are already perfect manifestations of the Universe happening exactly the way we are meant to happen. We are the manifestation of the energy of the Universe, in the form of a human being. We don't have to try to be anything because we are the perfect manifestation of the Universe, just the way we are. We don't have to try to be any particular way because we are the way the Universe created us to be.

There is nothing wrong with us, there never has been, there never will be, and there is nothing wrong with anyone or anything else, either. We are all perfect manifestations of the Universe, in human form. We can accept or we can reject the way we are. When we reject we stimulate conflict in us and with others. When we accept, we stimulate harmonious energy in us and in our relationships with one another.

When we accept everyone and everything, as it is, life becomes easy. When we accept our self, we relax into our own responses, how we really are, what we are really feeling, what attracts us, what excites us, what pleases us. When we accept our own responses, we can allow them to guide us. When we tune in to our own responses, we bypass the ideas, beliefs and stories of our society and we can enjoy our own experience of life. The socially fabricated pictures, ideas, beliefs and stories are just some conceptual view that we learned from our society and we can let it go and live in the moment with our own experience, that is happening in this and every moment.

When we accept our own responses as they are, we relax into our self and the ever-changing responses that our life is, that we are. When we accept ourselves, we are just here having what we are having and we are centered in our self and centered in the Universe. The Universe is everything that is happening and we are the Universe, along with everything and we are all happening, simultaneously. Acceptance allows us to allow reality to be the way it is and in the process we leave the socially fabricated illusion and shift our focus of attention on acceptance, harmony and enjoyment.

The Tsen Tsen Ming, an ancient Chinese text says "the great way is easy, for those with no preferences". When we accept all of life, just as it is, we are not struggling with any of it, not trying to change it, not trying to control it and life is easy and harmonious. Accepting reality, as it is, sets us free from the illusion that there is something wrong with someone or something, releasing us from the illusions of how we think we should be.

We can only create a different experience by letting go of our socially fabricated views about how we should be. When we accept our body, our mind, our feelings, our sensations as they all are, including all of the parts that we have been taught to reject, our vagina, our penis, our clitoris, our nipples, our breasts, our testicles, our anus, our lips, our tongue, our sensations, our feelings, our sexual sensations, our orgasms, our images, our fantasies, our thoughts, our anger, our fear, our sadness, our love, our sensuality, our sexuality, our desire, just as it all is, we free ourselves to be how we really are.

CHAPTER 67

We Are How We Are

——— ✿ ———

WE ARE HOW WE ARE and we are each having our own unique responses, our own feelings, our own sensations, our own thoughts, our own visions, our own fantasies, our own desires, our own wants, our own needs, our own expression, our own inclinations, our own perceptions, our own view and our own experiences.

We are each uniquely how we are, how we were designed to be and how we are supposed to be. We are the way were designed to be physically, emotionally and energetically. We can only experience our own experience and when we are centered in our own responses, our feelings, thoughts, and sensations and accepting and allowing them, we relax into the way we really are. When we accept and allow our own responses to be how they are, we can also accept and allow others to be the way they are.

Our unique responses are our personal guide to what fits for us, what resonates with us, what is in harmony with us, what we really want, what we really desire, what we really like, what we really enjoy, what really pleases us, and what really fulfills us.

Acceptance and allowance is the way to harmony, freedom and full self expression of our being. Acceptance is the key to harmony inside our self and and out side in our relationship with others.

We are each a perfect manifestation of life and we are each having our own unique experience of it and when we accept and allow everyone and everything to be, as it is, we come into harmony with reality, as it is.

CHAPTER 68

Centering

—◦∞◦—

CENTERING IN OUR SELF, IN our own energy, in our own experience is essential if we are to make decisions connected to what
is actually happening in us, to our own inner guidance. There
are many ways to learn to be centered and anything that helps
us center is valuable. Yoga and meditation train us to center in
our self, in our own energy, our own body, our own experience.
Yoga postures and breathing techniques are designed to focus
our attention inside our self, in the center of our own experience. Yoga teaches us to center in our self, as we stand, sit, lay,
breath and move. As we learn to focus our attention in our self,
we come to be present with our own responses, and accept them
as they are.

Focusing in our self, centering in our self, being aware of the
flow of our own energy, our own feelings, sensations and being
aware of our own experience of life, as it is happening in us,
requires being centered in ourselves, being aware of our own
experience and shifting our attention, away from our socially
created mind movie and the conceptual illusions of our culture
and focusing on our own individual energy.

The fundamental practice of yoga and meditation is learning to focus our attention on our own energy and be present with this energy that is moving in us continuously. Centering our attention in our own energy, rather than the movie in our mind, requires focus and practice.

Once we calm down and allow ourselves to focus on our own energy and be aware of the feelings, sensations, images and thoughts we are having, we are able to be with whatever is moving in us and through us and the movie in our mind begins to disappear. When we do focus fully on the energy that is within us, the mind movie stops playing of how we are supposed to be and our patterns of hiding and suppressing stops while all the sensations, feelings, thoughts, images, visions, fantasies, continue flowing through us.

Our energy is always moving in us in the form of sensations. Being centered allows us to let go of the mind movie and the patterns of hiding and suppressing that have taken over. The movies in our mind about how we "should be" begin to subside and in time we settle into our own energy and develop our ability to be present with our energy and it becomes easier to stay centered in our self. This develops our ability to be centered even when we are with others.

When we develop our ability to stay centered in our self our relating with others becomes easy and our relationships flow more freely and are the outcome of the open, honest expression of who and how we really are in each ongoing moment.

We have the extraordinary possibility of being how we really are and relating openly, honestly, freely and fully to one another and all that is required is our ability to be centered in our self and the ability to accept how we really are and the willingness to express our self freely.

Living beyond our beliefs is living in the reality of our own energy as it is flowing in us and through us with full awareness. Our energy is the energy of the Universe and it is moving in us and through us continuously and we can learn to be fully present with it and allow it to express honestly and openly. We are the energy of the Universe happening and when we allow this energy to flow freely we realize we are perfect manifestations of the Universe in human form.

Centering in our self and accepting this simple truth is all there is to do. Centering in our self and accepting our self, as we are, is the only thing we need to do or can do to get us out of the socially fabricated conceptual movie and the struggle it creates. When we center in our self and accept every aspect of our self as it is happening and realize we are the perfect manifestation of this energy, we see that there is nothing wrong with us and we see that we are the perfect manifestation of the Universe in human form.

CHAPTER 69

Being

———

"To be or not to be, that is the question". as Shakespeare said. Being who and how we really are is the answer to all of our conflicts. We simply have to be how we are and experience what we are experiencing and accept whatever that is and allow it to flow without criticism or judgement. Being is all. Being isn't trying to be some particular way according to some idea we have or trying to make something in particular happen. Being is allowing ourself to be how we already are before any mental assessments and accepting and allowing what is already happening within us to happen the way it is happening.

We learn to be by centering in our self and being with what is. There is no practice that is being but there are some practices that can support us in learning to be. Being is being with what is already happening in us and isn't the technique we are using to get here. Being is being with or without a technique. There is no doing. There is just being.

There is no answer in the usual sense of coming to a conclusion and having an answer and course of action to fulfill some intention. There is no answer in that sense. Being is just being with what is in us and around us.

CHAPTER 70

Our perfection

———— ∞∞∞ ————

WE ARE ALL PERFECT, EXACTLY the way we are and when we center in our self and accept our self completely, the way we are, we are able to be who we really are and how we really are and we begin enjoying our experience, whatever it is. In centering in our self and accepting our own perfection we relax into our real self and allow our self to be how we are and we begin to enjoy ourselves thoroughly and feel satisfied and fulfilled by our own experience. When we center in our self and accept the energy that is moving in us we see our own perfection and we can see the perfection of others and we can enjoy us and them for how we are and how they are and we can enjoy our relationship with everyone as it moves and changes into more relaxed interactions of mutual enjoyment.

The ultimate realization is self realization that comes with centering in our self and realizing we are all perfect just as we are. We are all having our own experience of reality and we each have the power to focus our attention on the energy that is always happening in us or on the mind movie and thus change our experience of reality. This simple act of centering in our self gives us each the power to tune into our own experience and frees us from the idea that our experience is being caused by someone or something outside of us. This awareness frees us from the illusion that we are slave to our upbringing or our socially fabricated illusions and makes us aware that we are in charge of our focus of attention and that our life is in our hands, based on our focus of attention.

Being who we really are in a world of illusion is the most important task that we can accomplish in our lives because it brings us into an awareness of our own energetic experience and gives us the power to be aware of our individual experience. We are the only one having our experience and the only one who can center in our experience and follow the guidance it is giving us to what is most resonant with us, with who we really are and what we are really experiencing.

We are each unique in every way and we are each having our own unique energetic responses to life and when we tune in to our self, into our own energy, we are impeccably guided to what is right for us, what is most resonant with us, what is truly in harmony with who we really are. When we tune into our self we are able to guide our own life toward what is in alignment with who we really are. In this way we take charge of our life by centering in our self, in our own energy and following the guidance that our own inner being is giving us in each moment.

CHAPTER 71

Acceptance

———— ∞ ————

ACCEPTANCE IS A DECISION WE must make for ourselves. We must make the decision to accept our self and others the way we actually are as a clear decisive choice. Accepting our self and everyone and everything, changes our way of seeing, our way of being and our way of relating to one another and life. When we accept our self, the way we are, every molecule, every cell, every body part, every emotion, every sensation, every image, we vibrate energetically with the energy of acceptance and the energy of acceptance emanates from us and is felt by others. When we accept our self, we relax into who and how we are and we let go of the ideas and beliefs. When we accept our self, we feel okay, because we are okay with our self and we are okay with others. When we accept our self and everyone the way we all are, we feel no conflict and we create no conflict because we are accepting, everyone the way we all are.

Accepting ourselves the way we are, in all of our unique and differing ways of being, removes the cause of conflict completely. Acceptance is the only thing that will ever bring us into harmonious relationship with our self and with one another, as we are, in all of our unique ways of being. Acceptance of our self and one another is the only cure for the conflict we are in, in our self and with one another. Acceptance opens us to our self and to one another and allows us to enjoy our own responses and our experiences with one another. Acceptance creates harmony and a feeling of trust and relaxation and opens us to being who and how we really are and supports us in relating openly, honestly, fully, freely and authentically. Acceptance allows us to be how we really are, whether we are alone or together. Accepting everyone and everything allows us to relax into our real self and our experience with one another.

When we accept our self and one another we relax into who we are and we relate with ease and comfort. Whether we are scarred, angry, sad, in love, or turned on sexually, we are okay with all of it when we are centered and accepting whatever that is.

We are how we are, everything is the way it is and when we accept reality as it is, we are at peace with it. I am how I am, you are how you are and everyone else is how they are. We aren't in charge and we can't change anyone. We just need to accept what is.

Acceptance is a decision that we must make in the face of all of our social conditioning to reject ourselves, to reject our own responses to reject our own energy. Making the decision to accept our self, changes our whole way of being and seeing our self and living our life centered in our self, in our own experience. We have to make this decision consciously to accept our self the way we really are, every feeling, every sensation, every thought, every vibration and when we accept what is, what we are experiencing and we vibrate with the energy of acceptance and this energy emanates from us and that is what others experience.

When we accept our self, we relax into our self, into our own responses and we leave the social belief that there is something wrong with us and we let go of the belief that there anything is wrong with anyone. When we accept our self, we are okay with our self. In accepting our own responses and accepting the responses of others, we accept everyone as they are and the conflict ends because we are accepting life as it really is by accepting our self as we really are.

Accepting the way we are, in all of our unique and differing ways of being, removes the causes of all conflict within us and with one another and we start allowing everyone and our allowing creates an atmosphere that allows everyone to be. Acceptance is the only thing we need to do to bring us into harmonious relationship with our self or one another, as we really are, in our unique ways of being and manifesting in human form.

Acceptance is the only cure for the conflict we feel in our self and with one another. Acceptance of our self as we really are, opens us to being how we really are and accepting our real responses and allowing them to be how they are and this allows us to enjoy our experiences with one another.

Acceptance creates a feeling of ease, trust and relaxation and opens us to accepting one another, openly, honestly and authentically, without the limitation and imposition of our learned socially fabricated ways of interacting.

When we accept how we really are, we accept others the way they really are and we stop trying to change our self or anyone else into being any other way then the way we are and this creates harmony in our relationships. Acceptance allows us to be how we really are, whether we are alone or with others.

Accepting our self and everyone else, allows us to relax into our self and into our experience with one another.

When we accept what is, life is easy, effortless, and enjoyable and whatever we are experiencing, we are okay with all of it. When we accept our self, accepting whatever that is in the form of feelings, sensations, thoughts, images, our body, everything about us we can relax into all of it and just have whatever we are having.

We are all created to be how we already are by the design of the Universe and when we accept our self, as we are, we experience peace with our self and therefor with others. I am how I am, you are how you are and everyone else is how they are and when we can accept this simple, basic truth we end conflict in our self and with everyone else.

64401906R00138

Made in the USA
Lexington, KY
07 June 2017